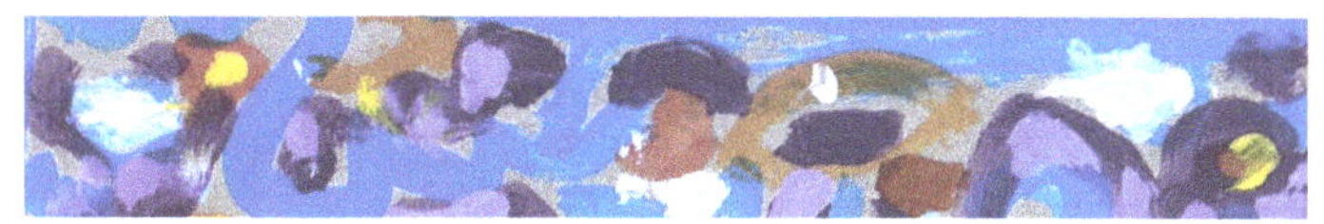

Realities of Life

Reflections in Verse

Alexander and Eva Peck

**Artwork by
Jindrich (Henry) Degen**

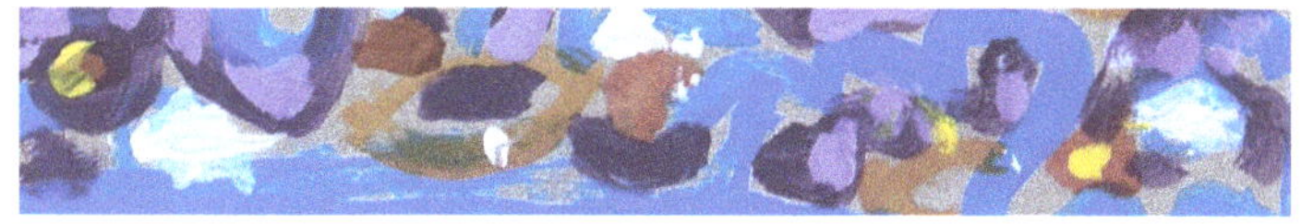

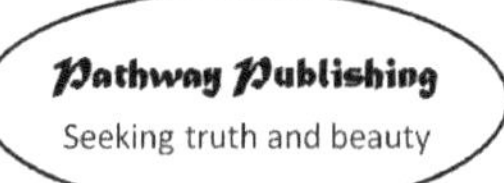
Pathway Publishing
Seeking truth and beauty

Dedication

To all readers

We wonder as we wander
Throughout this world
Of tragic strife
What is the answer to
The problems of life
The timeless answers
To our inner call
Love will transform us
One and all.

(C. Alexander Simpkins)

Life is not a problem to be solved, but a reality to be experienced.
(Soren Kierkegaard)

Life is a series of natural and spontaneous changes.
Don't resist them – that only creates sorrow.
Let reality be reality.
Let things flow naturally forward in whatever way they like.
(Lao Tzu)

The secret of success is learning how to use pain and pleasure
instead of having pain and pleasure use you.
If you do that, you're in control of your life.
If you don't, life controls you."
(Tony Robbins)

Contents

Preface

The poems in this book were first written, sometimes quickly, by Alex to capture insights about life that he had gained. Some of the thoughts came straight from his heart, in the peaceful early morning hours, spent reflecting on life over a cup of green tea. Others were inspired by reading and contemplation.

After sharing his first drafts with Eva, she masterfully edited them. Furthermore, she meaningfully added to the initial thoughts and reflections, greatly enhancing the original versions. She also drafted a few of the poems herself.

In compiling this collection, the intentions have been that as much as possible, the poems would be:

- Reality-based – true to lived experience.
- Inclusive – speaking to readers on any spiritual path, or none.
- Timeless – relevant today, next year, and in decades to come.
- Universal – able to touch people's lives across a broad spectrum.

However, while the poems are intended to speak to people of any spiritual orientation, readers may find a gentle undercurrent of Christian and/or Buddhist thought as a result of the background and studies by their authors.

Alex and Eva are pleased to have permission from Jindrich (Henry) Degen, Eva's father, to use some of his mainly abstract paintings as introductory pages to the sections and to the individual poems in this book.

The poems are arranged under the following themes:

- Truths of Life
- Wisdom for Life
- Acceptance
- End-of-Life Reflections
- In Memoriam
- Friendship
- Family
- On a Lighter Note

With the authors now well into their sixties, as well as having over the years been drawn to interact with and serve older members of their communities, the poems overall reflect a serious side of life. Specifically, four trains of thought have emerged: life has many wonderful qualities and is a precious opportunity to benefit oneself and many others; this life is impermanent and can end unexpectedly; life is inescapably governed by cause and effect; and life is not without difficulties, frustrations, and heartaches. To balance the soberness of the poems, Eva wisely suggested including a section entitled "On a Lighter Note"!

May readers find the feelings and thoughts about life captured in the poems helpful and insightful for their own life journey. Words, of course, are limited and so may they point to the deeper, heartfelt, and sometimes inexpressible, meanings.

Alex and Eva Peck
November 2017

Introduction

Since a number of the poems in this book touch on the end of life, dying, and the beyond, the following information may be helpful to understand our thrust.

The world's major religions agree that a kind and just life will lead to a peaceful and happy state after death. By contrast, a harmful and hateful life will bring harsh consequences, unless mitigated with positive actions while the opportunity exists (examples abound of sinners becoming saints).

Five aspects, indeed realities, of our life on earth are briefly described, to instruct and inspire:

- Life is a precious opportunity.
- Life is changeable and impermanent.
- Life situations are the consequences of actions.
- Life is marked by dissatisfaction.
- Life presents opportunities for us to realize our incredible human potential, both now and in the hereafter.

Life Consists of Precious Time

We need to understand how precious this life is. When spent wisely, life offers an opportunity to progress toward fulfilling our ultimate grand potential. Sadly, it is also easy to squander or neglect this chance, by only becoming absorbed in material pursuits.

Realistically, human life is both rich with enjoyments and attainments, and subject to many forms of suffering – physical, mental, and emotional. However, as we learn lessons and transform obstacles, life provides us with opportunities to enhance not just this life for ourselves and others, but also to sow the seeds for realizing our greatest potential.

Life Is Impermanent

When we reflect on our mortality and the impermanence of everything around us, a sense of urgency arises – an earnestness to make the most of the time we have in life, and not waste a moment.

We all know that our own end will arrive – but no one knows how or when (and it may arrive without warning). Yet, it's easy to slip into thinking that our life will last for quite a while yet – or that somehow it will remain as it is "forever".

But the fact is that we stay alive only as long as our mind/soul resides as a guest in the body, and there are many things that can quickly sever this temporary union.

We know at an intellectual level that if we fail to prepare for death and the hereafter, when the time comes, we will regret it – and by then it will be too late. If only we could bring this understanding from our head to the heart.

Life Circumstances Are Created by Our Actions

A strong incentive for not neglecting the spiritual side of life is deeply realizing that we will reap the fruits of our intentions, words and actions. This is the principle of karma.

Karma is not fate. Nor is it punishment meted out to us by an external agent or a Higher Power. We create our own karma by the choices we make every moment of each day.

When we pass through the gates of death, our karma is all we take with us – the results of our actions of body, speech, and mind, imprinted in our mind/soul. All else we enjoyed in life will be left behind. In a sense, death is an equalizer in that any wealth, fame, and beauty enjoyed, or poverty, obscurity, and pain endured, will be irrelevant.

If we are convinced of karma, we'll seize the present moment to build a good future life. Since intentions precipitate words and actions, we need to be constantly mindful of our mental attitudes to ensure that they are loving, compassionate, joyful, and equanimous.

Life Is Marked by Dissatisfaction

While all of us long for happiness, we find that this world is filled with pain and ultimately unsatisfying.

All around us, we can see suffering such as heartbreak, depression, illness, and grief. Also, we suffer when separated from what we hold dear, when encountering what is undesirable, and when not achieving what we want even after pursuing it. These universal forms of pain have been described as "blatant suffering."

Upon a closer look, we will notice another kind of suffering that tints our joy and satisfaction: an underlying fear that all good things will end or change. No matter how beautiful and pleasurable our surroundings and enjoyments, our situation cannot possibly remain as it is. It is bound to change because it is not beyond the law of impermanence. This second form of suffering has been called the "suffering of change."

Finally, and this needs to be deeply contemplated for its inevitable reality to sink in, death will appear at our door. The elements of our physical body will merge with those of the earth. Only our mind/soul continues on.

The Great Potential of Life

From experience, if we observe closely, we may notice that many people are by nature loving, peaceful, and wise. Also, disasters often bring out the best in people as strangers sacrificially assist those affected – desiring to alleviate suffering at all costs. Sometimes people risk their lives to save others. We begin to open to the possibility that a basic goodness dwells in all humans.

If this is so, then there is no one who cannot, under the right conditions, become aware of the qualities of basic goodness in their heart – which so often lies buried and dormant. Our negative emotions and unhealthy habitual tendencies are just afflictions – mental poisons – not our true nature. They are like dark clouds temporarily obscuring the brilliant sun.

We all have a choice. If we become aware of, and then nurture, our basic goodness – for example, the love, compassion, joy, equanimity, peace, and wisdom within – this will transform our life. Unhappy situations will affect us less and less. However, if we fail to make the most of our life now, then in the future we will inevitably fall into the misery of fear, pain, and confusion.

Looking at life as it is, may we begin to realize that to attain our highest potential, we must pursue a spiritual path. It can be any path that encourages the cultivation of the love, compassion, and wisdom within; that loosens the grip on our continual grasping; that helps the release of our mental poisons; that purifies our minds; and that refines our words and deeds. This is the only way to reach a fully enlightened state in our future life that will be satisfying and forever free of pain and suffering.

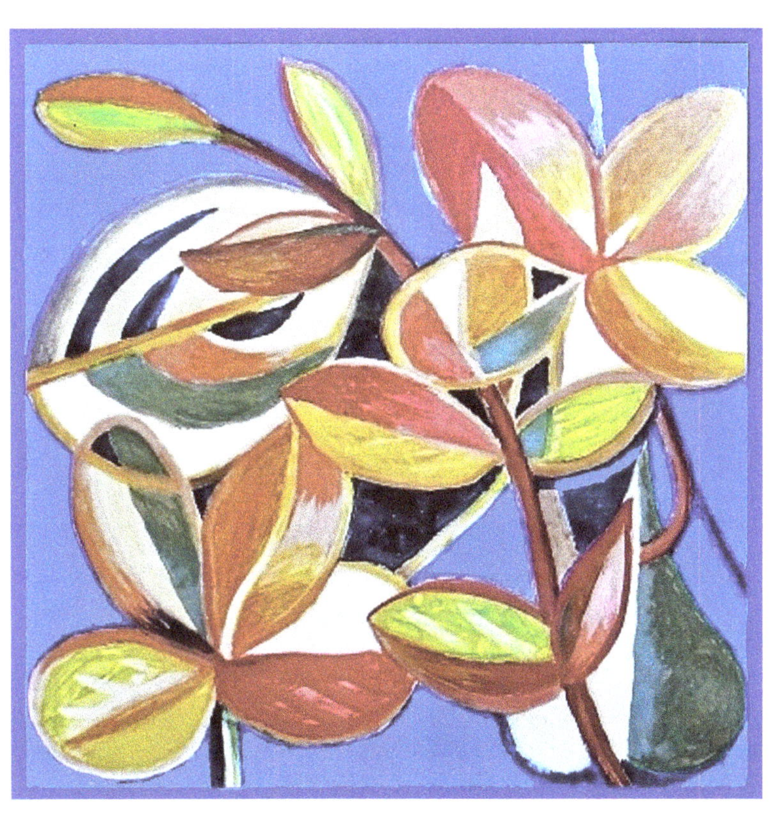

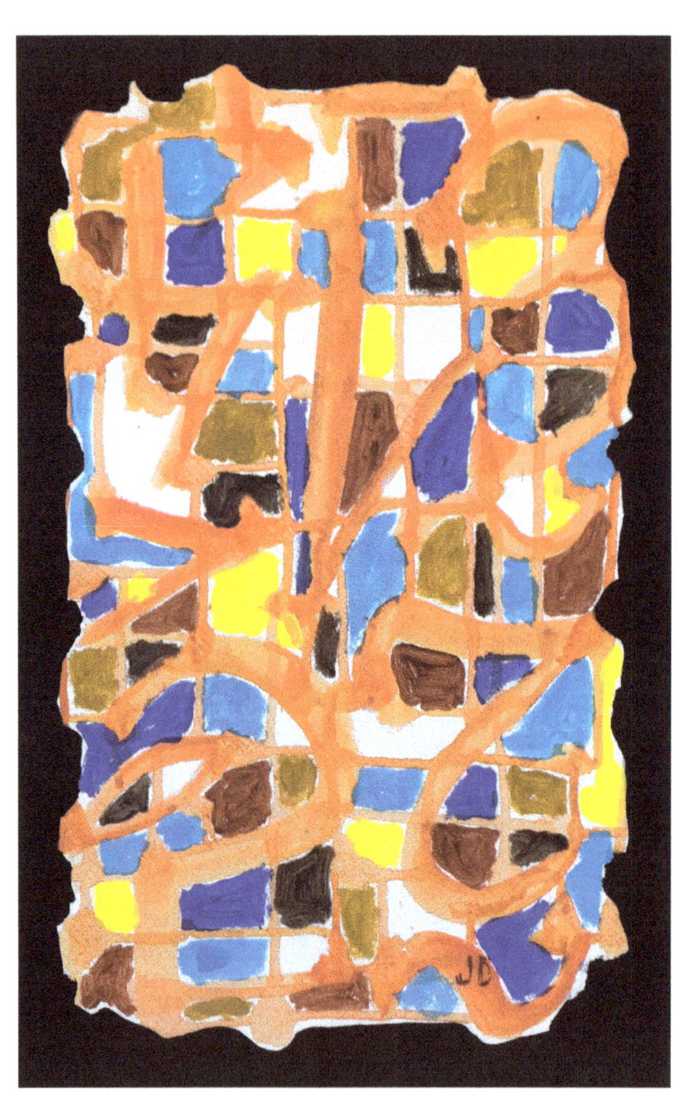

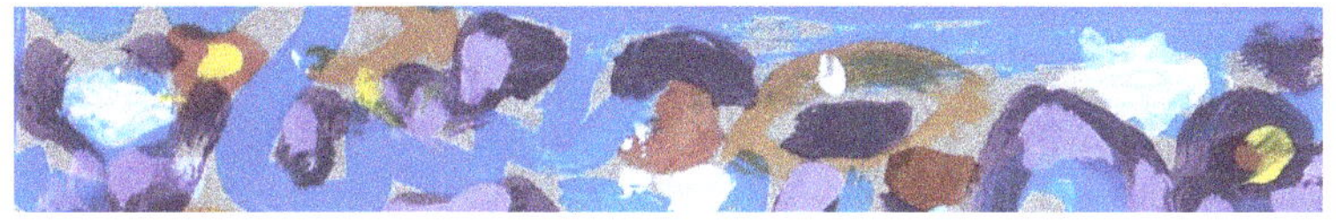

Truths of Life

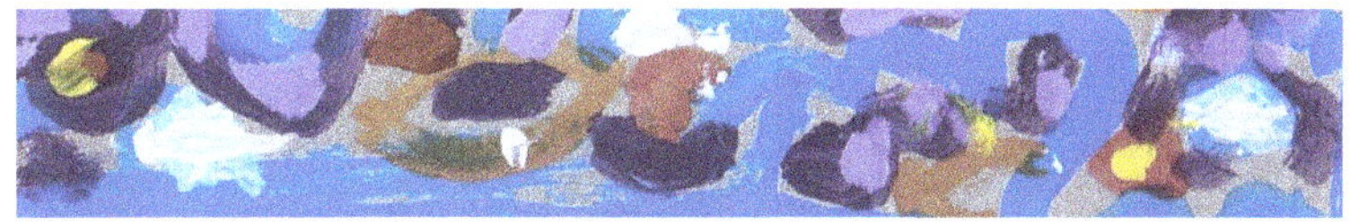

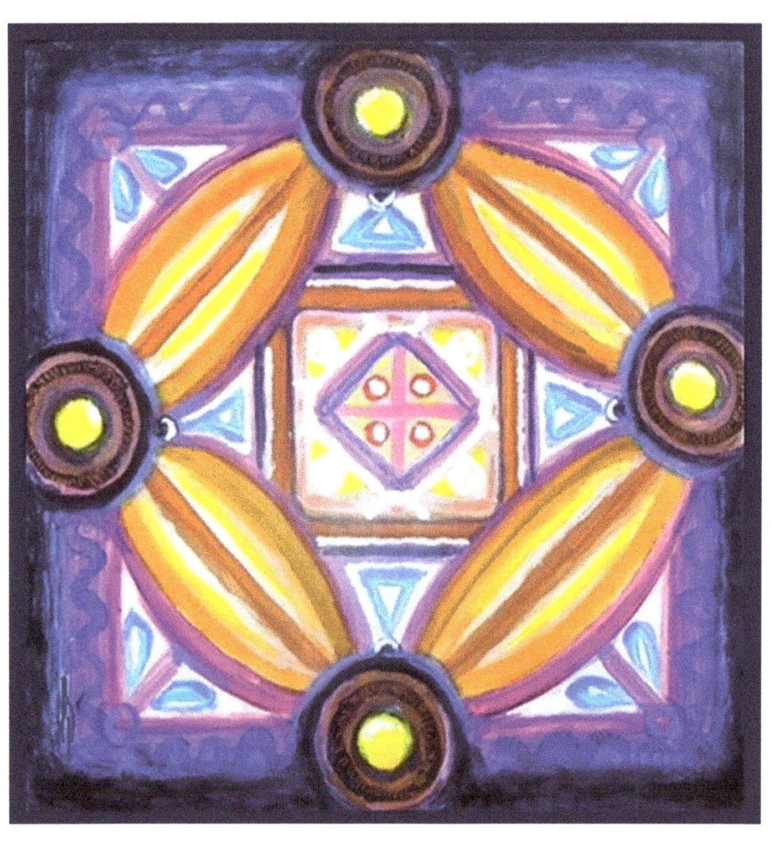

Four Realities

We have many favourable conditions in the present;
Let's make sure that our life is not misspent.
Wasting our precious life in trivial distraction
Would be the height of deceit and foolish action!

All things, like ocean waves, are impermanent;
And we never know when death our way will be sent.
Everything is constantly shifting and changing,
From body cells to galaxies, it's truly wide-ranging!

Life brings no lasting happiness, but stress;
People in the world face much fear and distress.
We also create suffering with our own minds;
So, we must free ourselves from these self-made binds.

We will ultimately reap what we sow;
So, we must act well for good results to show.
As it is often said, that whatever you do,
Will, in time, definitely come back to you.

These four realities are a part of human existence.
We need to accept what arises without resistance.
Needed is a Purpose bigger than you or me,
And a Path to eternally set us free!

While we are able, we must seize the day,
And bring a higher vision for life into play!
May our lives be of great benefit to each other;
And never our sublime potential with folly smother!

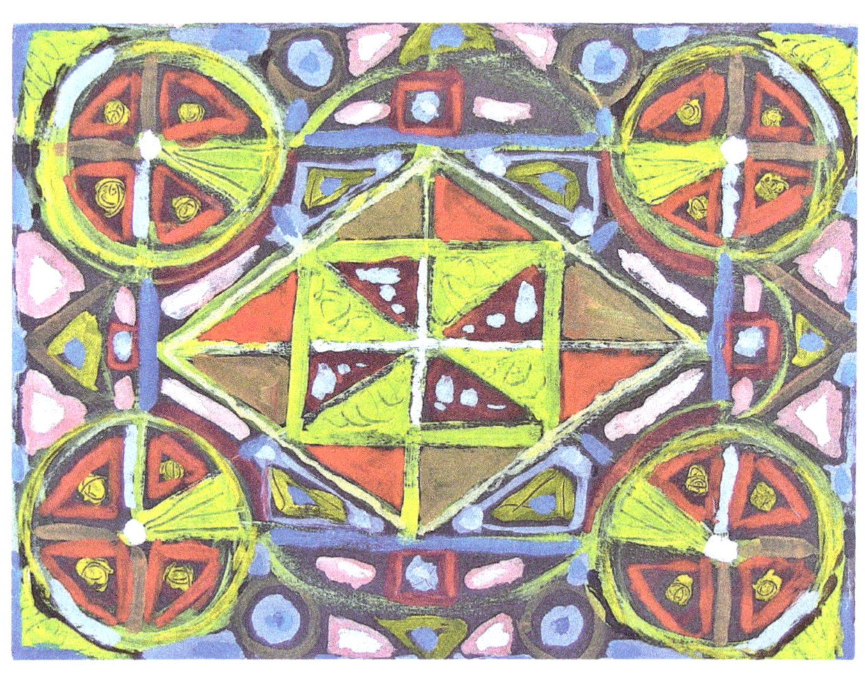

Four Facts of Life

A privileged life is like finding a treasure of jewels,
So, rejoice, benefit others; don't live like fools!
Now is your chance for many a wholesome deed;
Therefore live a good life and flee any misdeed.

The freedoms you have aren't always easy to find;
Make use of these, and to your potential don't be blind.
Now that you have such a favourable condition,
Use your talents well, and don't fall into perdition!

With each hour and each day, life is running out!
We must never forget that, and not just loll about.
This life is fleeting, like a bubble in a stream;
Here today, gone tomorrow, unreal as this may seem.

Our lives are indeed running out very fast;
There's no going back to what's now in the past.
We never know what first will arrive:
Tomorrow here or in another world be alive!

In this life, misfortune can unexpectedly strike;
We encounter enemies and things we do not like;
Losing what is pleasant and what we much admire;
And suffer from not getting what we badly desire.

In our life, from five deadly poisons we cannot hide:
Ignorance, craving, hatred, as well as jealousy and pride.
Suffering of various kinds is common to us all,
And without exception, death will everyone befall.

There is one truth, that understand we all need:
We create happiness or suffering by each and every deed.
The results of our actions ripen on us – that we know well;
Whether sooner or later, however, we cannot foretell!

This life may be short, but whether a decade or more years,
The result of our deeds in our future life certainly appears.
We must remember that effects will correspond to the cause;
So, before thoughts, words, and actions, for a moment we should pause.

These four realities are sobering indeed.
What can give us hope from them to be freed?
For refuge, we cannot rely on fame or praise or gain.
These eventually bring disillusionment again.

All true religions point us to a great sacred reality;
To deeply realize this gives us a special opportunity.
We also need to rely on inspired teachings,
To transcend this world's miseries and help other beings.

In this way only will we not stray and go amiss,
And live our lives in a way that brings eventual bliss.

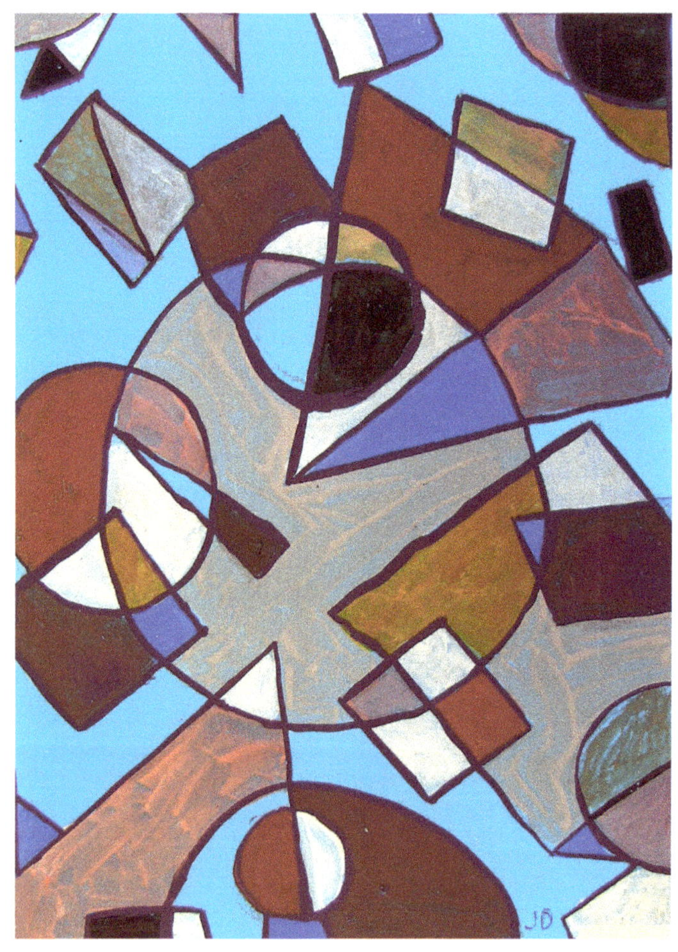

Such Is Life

Life's Opportunities

We have many favourable conditions in the present;
Let's make sure that our time is well spent.
Wasting our precious life in trivial distraction
Would be the height of deceit and foolish action!

A privileged life is like finding a treasure of jewels,
So, let's rejoice, benefit others; not live like fools!
Now is our chance for many a wholesome deed;
Therefore live a good life and flee any misdeed.

The freedoms we have aren't always easy to find;
Let's make use of these, and to our potential not be blind.
Now that you have such a favourable condition,
Use your talents well, and don't fall into perdition!

Impermanence

All things, like ocean waves, are impermanent;
And we never know when death our way will be sent.
Everything is constantly shifting and changing,
From body cells to galaxies, it's truly wide-ranging!

With each hour and each day, life is running out!
We must never forget that, and not just loll about.
This life is fleeting, like a bubble in a stream;
Here today, gone tomorrow, unreal as this may seem.

Our lives are indeed running out very fast;
There's no going back to what's now in the past.
We never know what first will arrive:
Tomorrow here or in another world be alive!

Suffering

Life brings no lasting happiness, but stress;
People in the world face much fear and distress.
We also create suffering with our own minds;
So, we must free ourselves from these self-made binds.

In this life, misfortune can unexpectedly strike;
We encounter enemies and things we do not like;
Losing what is pleasant and what we much admire;
And suffer from not getting what we badly desire.

In our life, from five deadly poisons we cannot hide:
Ignorance, craving, hatred, as well as jealousy and pride.
Suffering of various kinds is common to us all,
And without exception, death will everyone befall.

Karma

We will ultimately reap what we sow;
So, we must act well for good results to show.
As it is often said, that whatever you do,
Will, in time, without question return back to you.

There is one truth, that understand we all need:
We create happiness or suffering by each and every deed.
The results of our actions ripen on us – that we know well;
Whether sooner or later, however, we cannot foretell!

This life may be short, but whether a decade or more years,
The result of our deeds in our future life certainly appears.
We must remember that effects will correspond to the cause;
So, before thoughts, words, and actions, for a moment we should pause.

A Transcendent Purpose

These four realities are sobering indeed.
What can give us hope from them to be freed?
They indeed are certainties of the human existence.
We need to accept what arises without giving resistance.

For refuge, we cannot rely on fame or praise or gain.
These eventually will bring disillusionment again.
While we are still able, we must seize the day,
And bring a higher vision for life right here into play!

Needed is a Purpose bigger than you or me,
And a Path that beyond this life will eternally set us free!
May our lives be of benefit to ourselves and each other,
And never our sublime potential with senseless folly smother!

All true religions point us to a great sacred reality;
To deeply realize this gives us a special opportunity.
We also need to rely on inspired teachings,
To transcend this world's miseries and help other beings.

In this way only will we not stray and go amiss,
And live our lives in a way that brings eventual bliss.

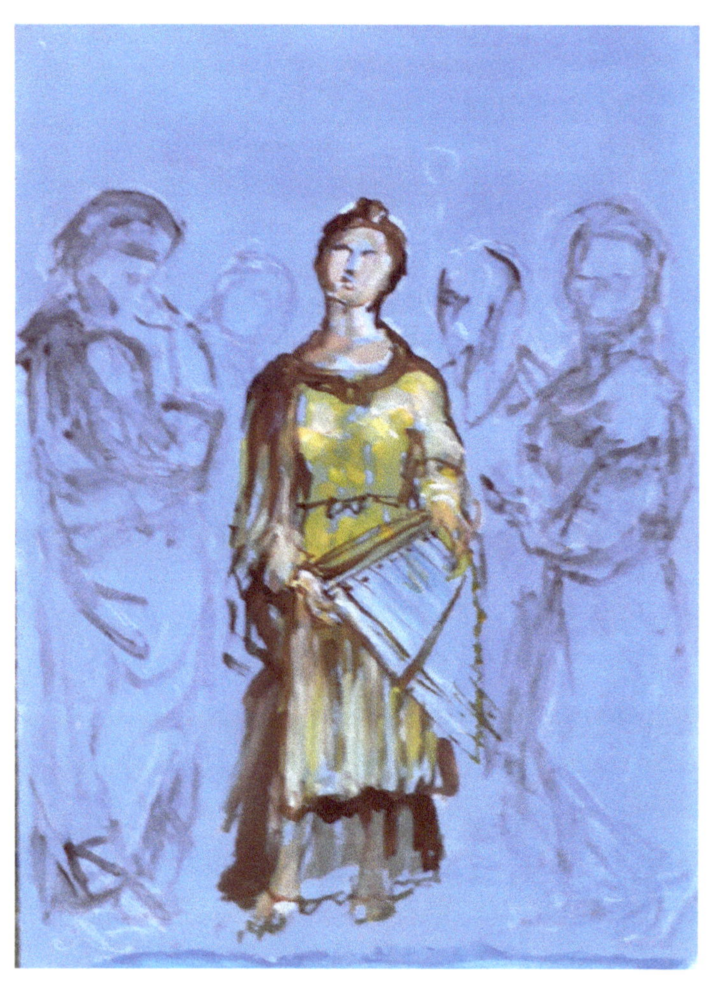

Precious Human Life

Born into fortunate conditions can't be taken for granted,
When so many live in circumstances far from enchanted!
Some spend their whole lives in abject poverty trapped,
Others in disability or poor health for many years strapped.

A privileged life is like finding a chest of jewels,
So let's be grateful, help others; not live like fools!
This is our chance for many a wholesome deed;
Hence, live a good life and strive to flee all misdeed.

Many favourable conditions we have in the present;
Therefore, we must ensure that our time is well spent.
To waste our precious opportunities in trivial distraction,
Would be the height of folly and unwise action!

The freedoms we have aren't always easy to find;
Maximize them we must, and to our potential not be blind.
If you find yourself in an advantageous condition,
Use your talents well, and do not fall into perdition!

Saints and sages down through the ages,
Have written about another life in their pages.
How we live life now will have a direct bearing,
On our state in the next life, they're declaring.

If many good conditions for us have coincided,
If we have good health and most needs provided,
Not a slave to another, but being independent,
Diligent we must be in seeking the transcendent!

Our precious opportunities in life can be easily lost,
We never know into what state we may be suddenly tossed!
Having a good life, one must never fall into contempt for others;
How foolish to be ignorantly judging our sisters and brothers!

Seeing its wonderful qualities, we can rejoice in this human life,
With its freedoms and conditions for spiritual practice rife!
This opportunity we must use well to benefit other beings,
Not take it for granted or waste it, but be clearly seeing!

Reflect on those who squander their life only on worldly goals;
Not giving the slightest thought to the state of their souls!
May they realize their earthly tenure is uncertain as a candle flame;
That family, friends, and possessions won't just continue all the same!

May all humans not endowed with spiritual inclinations,
Find opportunities to fulfil their highest aspirations.
May we make the best use of whatever our circumstances,
And not leave this life empty-handed, having lost precious chances!

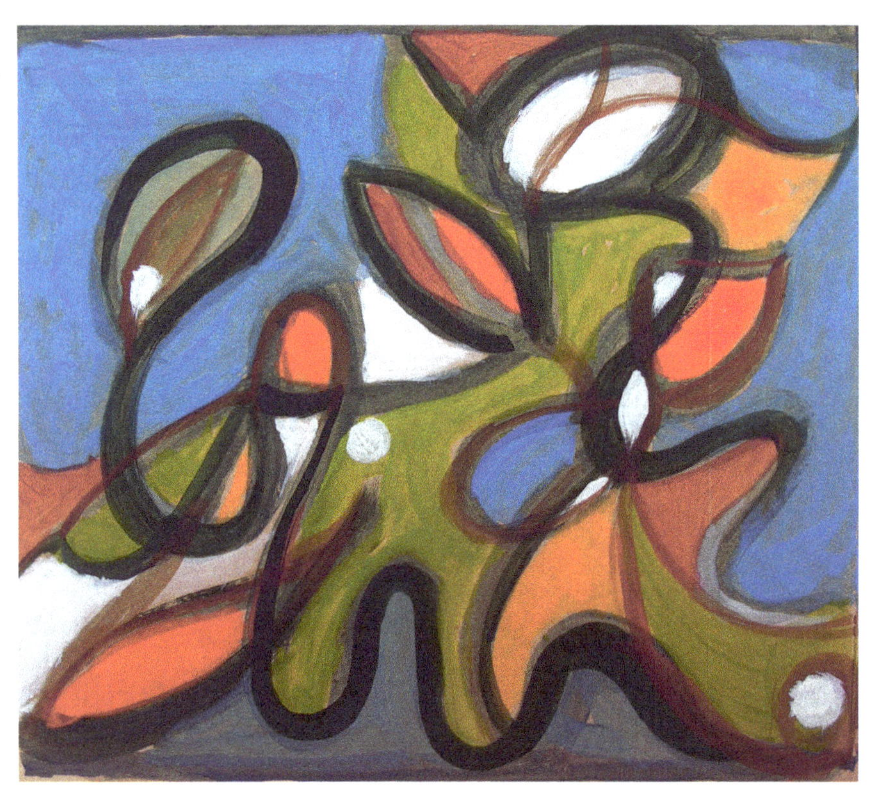

Impermanence

All around us and within, nothing stays the same.
The only permanent thing is change in our life's game!
We go from birth, via childhood, teen years, adulthood to older age;
But, never know when death will come, as told by many a sage.

In our lives, people and physical things come and go.
We're all part of a continual change and never-ending flow!
Many of our friends and relatives have gone their separate ways,
Even though we had spent with them a lot of lovely days.

Each life has its ups and downs, that much is for sure.
And we never know what may lie right behind our door!
Conflicts and resolutions belong to our life's walk;
And of both, many joys and sorrows we can inevitably talk.

Change surrounds us at every step – for everything there's a season;
What looks solid and enduring may seem to change without reason.
We all witness birth, growth, decline, and eventually death;
Such a display of ongoing change can take away one's breath!

Indeed, all things, like ocean waves, are impermanent;
And truly we never know when death our way will be sent.
Everything is constantly shifting and changing,
From cells to galaxies, it's amazingly wide-ranging!

With each hour and each day, our life is running out!
We must never forget that, and not just loll about.
This life is indeed fleeting, like a bubble in a stream;
Here today, gone tomorrow, unreal as this may seem.

For every one of us, time is going very fast;
And there's no going back to what's now in the past.
In addition, we never know what will first arrive:
Tomorrow here, or in another world we may be alive!

So, deep within, we yearn for what's permanent at its kernel.
May we each find that which is truly everlasting and eternal!
In the meantime, many favourable conditions exist in the present;
So seize the day, savour every moment, before our time is spent!

By ourselves we can only do so much,
From a Higher Power we do need a touch.
That Love exists in the Universe can be seen beyond human free will;
Our souls can be transformed by this Love if we can stop and be still.

Ask and you shall receive, we have read;
Father is always willing to give his children bread –
The Bread of Life which transforms us and gives immortality.
Who would want to forgo such a great opportunity?

Each year, month, week, day, hour and minute, our lives shorter grow;
If we fritter time away in trivia, we'll have nothing in the end to show.
Every thought, word, and action sown counts now and in the hereafter;
May we forever through Love harvest happiness, filled with joyful
laughter.

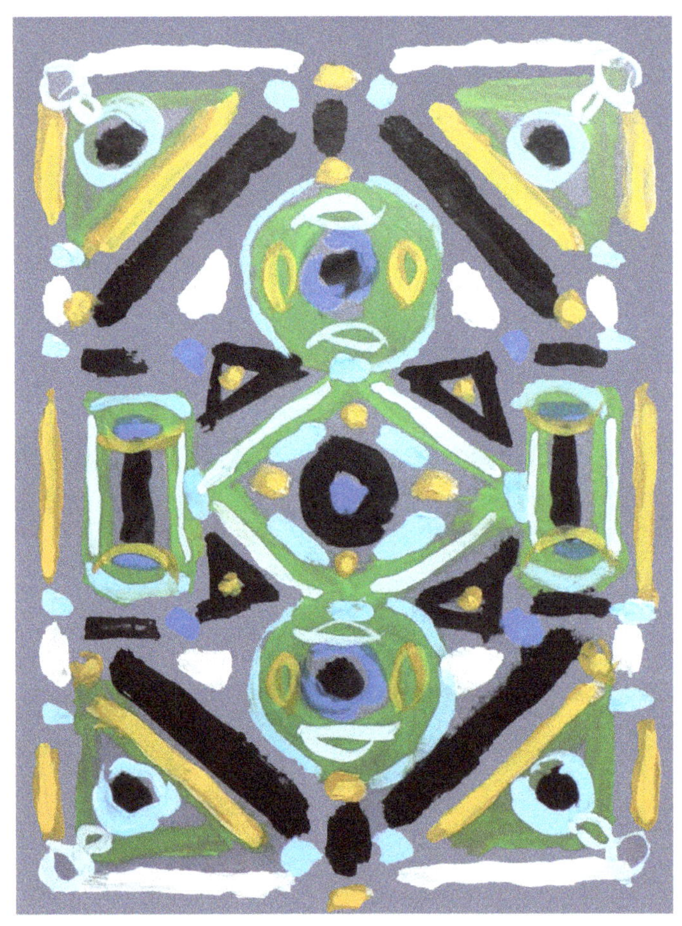

Here Today – Gone Tomorrow

Not far from us is a scenic Golf Club by the sea;
Its bistro receptionist, Judy, was always friendly.

As lunch guests, we'd be greeted with a kind, warm smile.
This helped make going there, besides the food, worthwhile.

Over the years, Judy was almost always there.
A brief chat, a quote, or even a poem we'd share.

For birthdays, Judy ensured our enjoyment with a special touch.
She arranged our table to be just right; nothing was too much.

Recently, we went back to that special Golf Club by the sea,
But this time, Judy at the reception desk we did not see.

So, we asked one of the staff members about Judy.
She has gone on, they told us, praising her truly.

"Here today, gone tomorrow"– these words struck a chord in my heart.
A lesson of life dawned on me: From all in this life we must each part.

How true the words about impermanence by the great Indian sages;
They show the reality of all things physical throughout the ages:

"Whatever is born is subject to death and dying.
Whatever rises will fall and end on the ground lying.

Whatever is gathered will disperse and scatter.
What comes together will separate and no longer matter."

A seed sprouts and grows into a plant, but in time will wither and die;
In youth full of energy we feel, but we, too, will perish by and by.

Empires rose and flourished, but now lie in ruins under desert sands;
We work hard to succeed, but in old age struggle with shaky hands.

Food prepared is gone after guests have enjoyed their stay;
Money hard-earned and saved will all go to others one day.

Parents must let go of their children when they have grown up;
At life's end, we will part from everyone, even the lovable pup!

Being with friends also changes; the time always comes to part;
May we take this to heart, before it is time to depart.

It's good to grasp that every relationship is marked by transience,
Even with our loved ones; such is the reality of existence.

Sadness is natural when one experiences a loss of some kind;
But to the fact that nothing is permanent we mustn't be blind.

Remembering the transitory nature of things is helpful indeed,
When we suffer loss or part from friends and the heart does bleed.

May we see that everything continuously flows and changes;
And not think that all will continue exactly the same for ages.

We may be sad, and even suffer, when things that we like change;
But, change is good, even though this may to us sound strange!

Thanks to impermanence, everything, including new life, is possible!
If children didn't grow up, future generations would be impossible.

If a seed did not change into a tree, no fruit to eat would mature;
By seeing the miracle of impermanence, our grief can be less for sure.

So, while sad at first not to have Judy greet us from her work station,
We wish her further growth and flourishing in her new location.

For all of us who may presently grieve or be disheartened by a change,
May we see transience as good, even though it can sound strange.

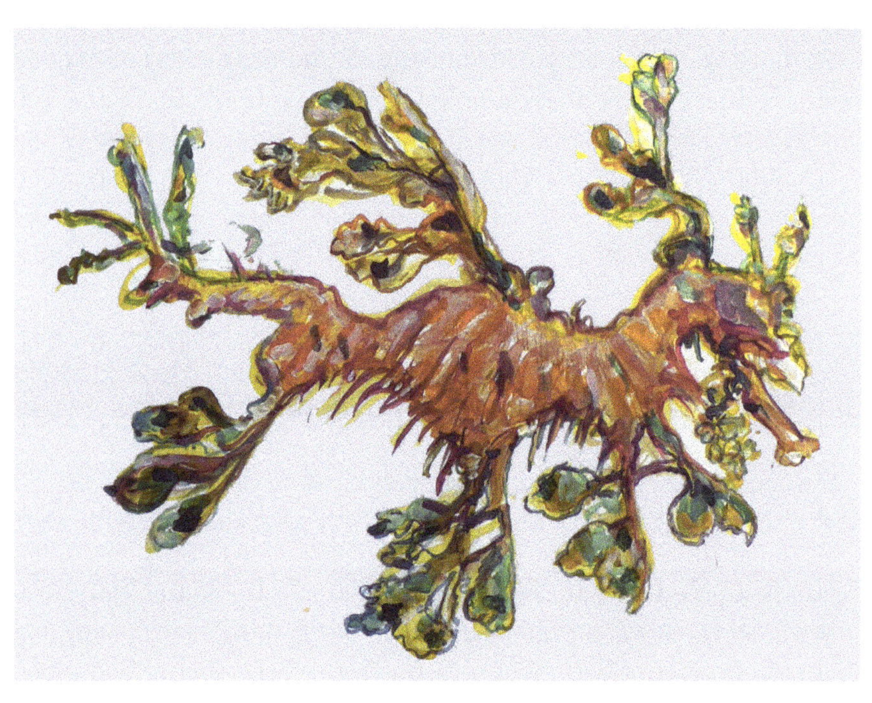

Ocean of Suffering

Life brings many troubles and a lot of stress;
People around the world face much fear and distress.
In this life, misfortune can unexpectedly strike;
We encounter enemies and things we do not like.

We lose what is pleasant and what we much admire;
And suffer from not getting what we badly desire.
We also create suffering with our own minds;
So, free ourselves we should from these self-made binds.

From five deadly poisons in our life we cannot hide:
Ignorance, craving, hatred, as well as jealousy and pride.
Suffering of various kinds is common to us all,
And without exception, death will everyone befall.

Though we want to be at peace and happy,
Our actions often cause us to be unhappy!
And, though we'd like to avoid or escape from suffering,
Its causes we practice, and reap the bad results they bring!

All human beings long to free themselves from misery,
But in unwise deeds persist, and then cry out for delivery!
Indeed, they long for joy, but in their ignorance,
Destroy joy, the same as they would a foe or hindrance!

All things that we possess and use, so real and tangible seem;
Yet, seen from life's end, they're like a fleeting vision or dream.
All that we cling to will fade into the realms of memory,
And never again in the same way exist or come to be.

We need to imagine ourselves in a place of human suffering,
Such as being caught in a war zone with no one delivering,
Constant fear of being maimed or killed, everywhere devastation,
Separation from family and friends, inhumanity to man and isolation.

Countless people in the world are caught in cycles of misery,
With no idea how to extricate themselves and no hope of delivery.
Ponder their predicament until compassion and tears well up,
With a burning wish that their suffering be taken from their cup!

In sum, many are the miseries of life in which we wallow.
Without transcendent purpose, this world alone is hollow.
It's good to reflect on the suffering common to all,
The miseries of earthly existence which us befall.

To begin, suffering surrounds our coming to this earth,
The struggle and pain which accompanies childbirth.
Then miseries of illness and disease will often occur,
Frustration and anxiety will us from pleasant things deter.

Later, the sufferings of old age begin to show,
Lack of energy and physical decline may come as a blow.
Finally, there is the misery of death with its separation –
From wealth, influence, family, friends, and then cessation.

Even if today our life seems happy and we possess much –
A healthy body, house, money, family, friends and such,
These all remain uncertain and may be short-lived to our surprise;
Because of inherent impermanence, the suffering of change will arrive.

Indeed, this earthly human realm has no scarcity of affliction;
So we need to pursue a higher, more lasting vision with conviction.
Also, if we can stand in others' shoes, exchanging ourselves with them,
Then we'll deeply long for enlightenment for all, and no-one condemn!

We cannot rely on the passing and fleeting happiness of this world,
Perhaps a wealthy, peaceful existence, and a life that is pearled!
If we do, dismay and discontent will sooner or later be our lot.

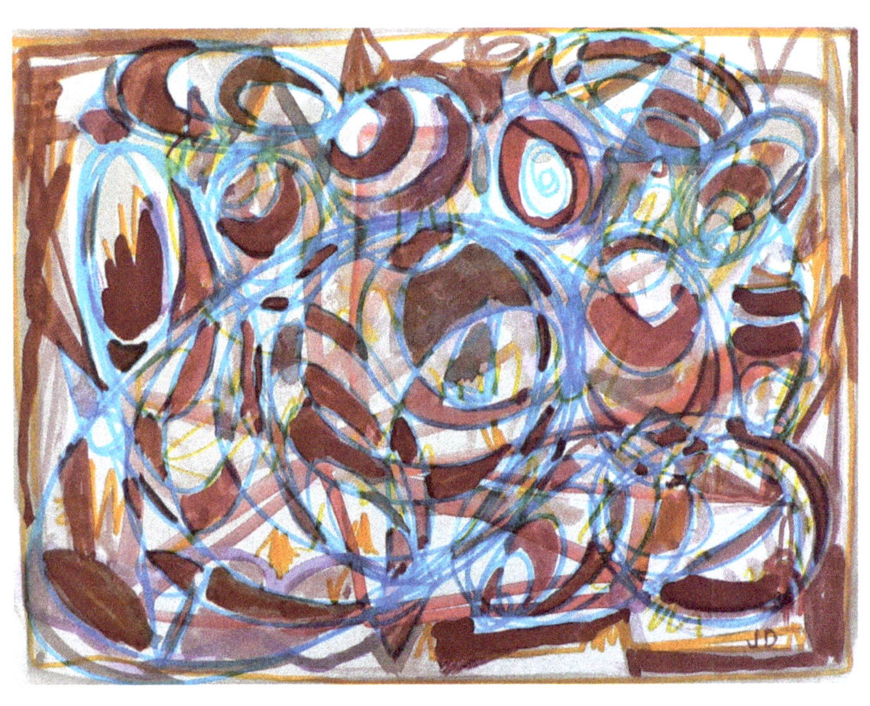

Sowing and Reaping

The truth of "karma" to know and understand we all need:
We can create happiness or sorrow by each and every deed.
Results of our actions ripen on us, as some have learned well;
Exactly how and when, however, we cannot always tell!

We will ultimately reap what in this life we sow;
So, we must act the best we can for good results to show.
As is often rightly said, that whatever you do,
Will, in time, without a doubt return back to you.

So, we should ponder our intent, action, as well as the effect.
Motivation is what prompts us an act outward to direct.
The action can be a thought, word, or deed that we set in motion;
The effects of our intents and acts may be as vast as the ocean!

In this life, intention, action and result can't be fully understood;
But, the following sums it all up in a way that is sound and good:
Kind intents and wise deeds tend to bring a fine outcome;
Mean aims and harmful acts often yield trouble for one.

It's true that although doing wrong or evil deeds,
May not at once, like a sword, create a gash that bleeds.
Yet, in the life beyond, the result of those acts will show;
Their karmic fruit clearly will be revealed and to us flow.

Even though happiness may come in this life through many an evil deed,
This will only lead to immense suffering in the after-life indeed!
In this life, the exact working of karmic results cannot be clearly shown.
But, the reality of the law of cause and effect is to all of us well known!

Hurting a person "for their own good", while pure in intention,
Is an example of an inappropriate and disagreeable action.
To give and serve a needy cause, wanting just praise and recognition,
While benefit it will bring to some, is not an honourable motivation.

Positive or negative, even though a deed may seem negligible,
At its maturation, the result could be far from trivial!
One spark on a hot summer's day can set ablaze an entire forest;
An ill-chosen word or remark can for years give a person no rest!

We should seek through kind intention,
Well-chosen words, and disciplined action,
To create causes and conditions for a good situation,
And not blame bad fate for what's our own causation!

May we not seek gratification just for the moment,
Then blame our trouble on others with a lament.
Instead, may we have a long-term view of cause and effect,
And, thinking of karmic results, seek our behaviour to perfect!

In sum, from good aims and actions, happiness will ultimately result,
Negative intents and deeds will us sooner or later into misery catapult!
To do the former and avoid the latter, we are responsible;
Though, exactly how they'll ripen, for us to know isn't possible.

So thoroughly assess our karmic situation we must,
Appraising the priorities of this life and its thrust.
Also, review we should our karmic patterns from the past,
And see what our present intentions and actions forecast.

This life may be short, but whether a decade or more years,
The result of our deeds in our future life certainly appears.
We must recall that effects will follow the intention and deed;
So, let's to our thoughts, words and actions give good heed!

There is a glorious state and realm about which many have not heard,
And visions and concepts of this are often in understanding blurred.
Yet finally, the reality of the law of karma, beyond ideas of time,
Will be transcended in an ultimate realm that is man's destiny sublime!

But, even if we may have insights into this inexpressible, future glory,
The law of cause and effect is still very much a part of our story!

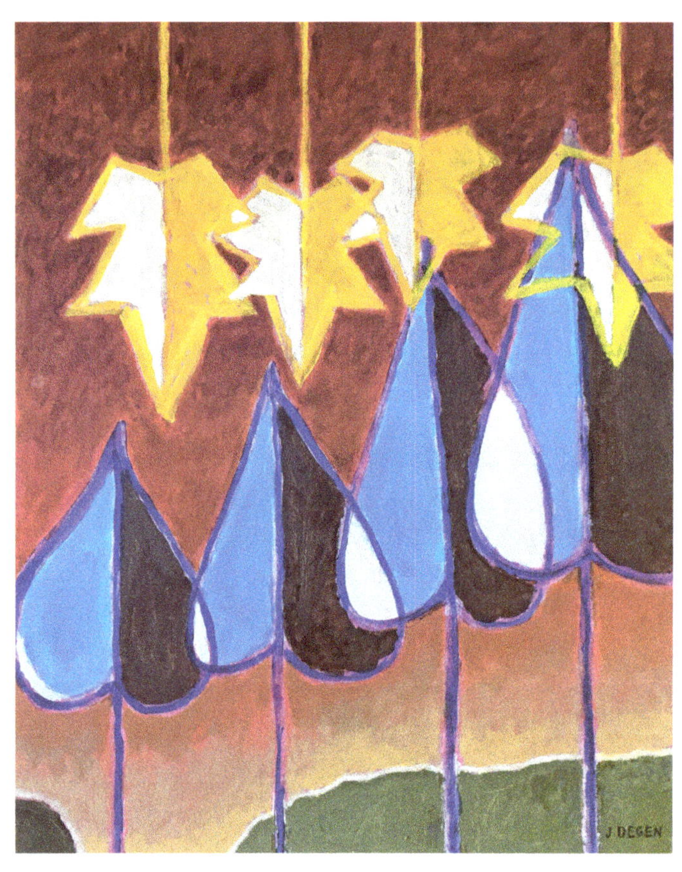

J DEGEN

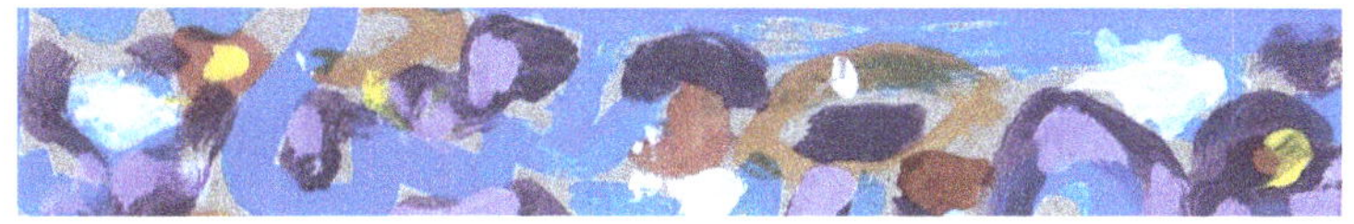

Wisdom for Life

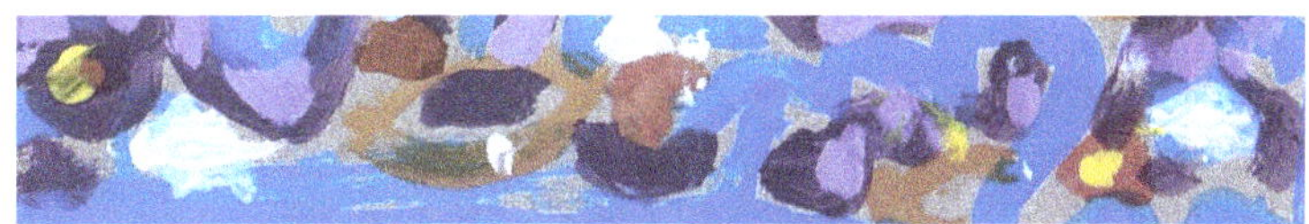

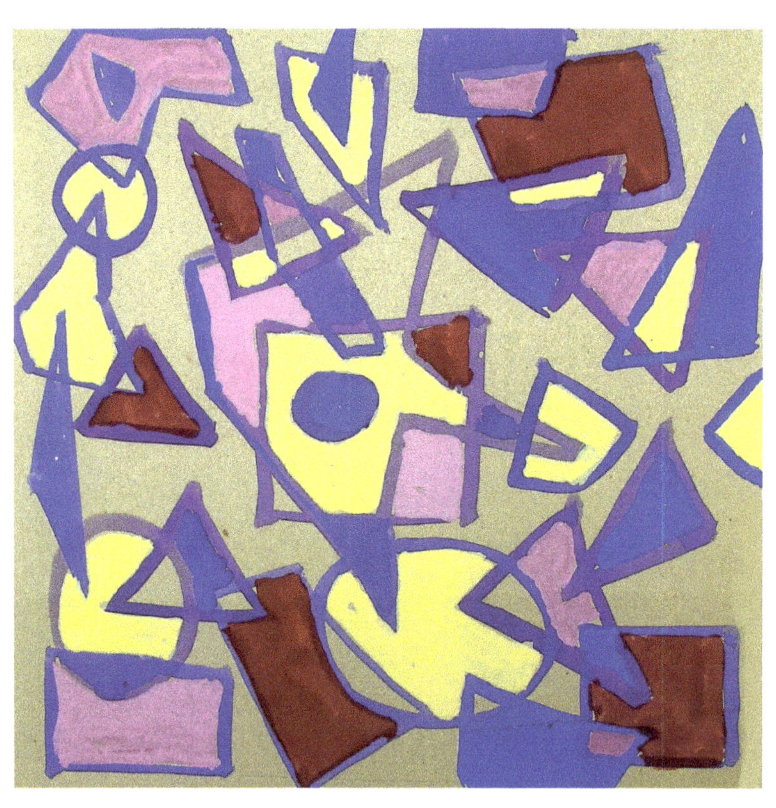

On Seeking the Truth

To find a true path in life is not an easy task,
So for effort from us we must diligently ask.
Four principles will help you greatly on the way,
Let them guide your heart and mind each and every day!

We cannot just rely on a teacher,
Even if great charisma is their feature!
Freedom from suffering comes from the truth that is taught,
So to the message we must give earnest thought.

Seek to understand what a person is deeply sharing,
Without about each word and expression unduly caring.
If we focus just on, and get lost in, every word,
The real meaning for us may not have been heard.

See what needs to be interpreted and is only implicit;
Better is taking to heart the sure and explicit.
Rely on teachings where the meaning is clear,
These will your life in a better direction steer.

Our thinking is limited and we understand fuzzily,
Then the light can break through, simply and easily!
When we can quieten our judgmental mind,
Insights and understanding soon we may find!

To ignore these four principles is a mistake,
Which on the wrong path easily can us take!
On name, fame, and just words, we can't stand,
Nor on what is far too simple to understand.

In the end, it is the truth that sets us free;
This applies to all people universally!
But by ourselves we can only do so much,
From a Higher Power we all need a touch.

We need help with getting understanding,
Else our truth search is without ending.
Round and round in circles we may go,
And the greatest insights and opportunities forgo.

Love and light exist in the cosmos beyond our human will;
We may be transformed by this, if we can reflect and be still.
Ask and you shall receive, we have heard and read,
This love will radically change us as on its path we tread.

The love will inevitably lead us to immortality.
May we not miss human life's grandest opportunity.
The way to the eternal and immortal is the greatest truth of all,
Above endless pain and suffering it'll lift us once and for all.

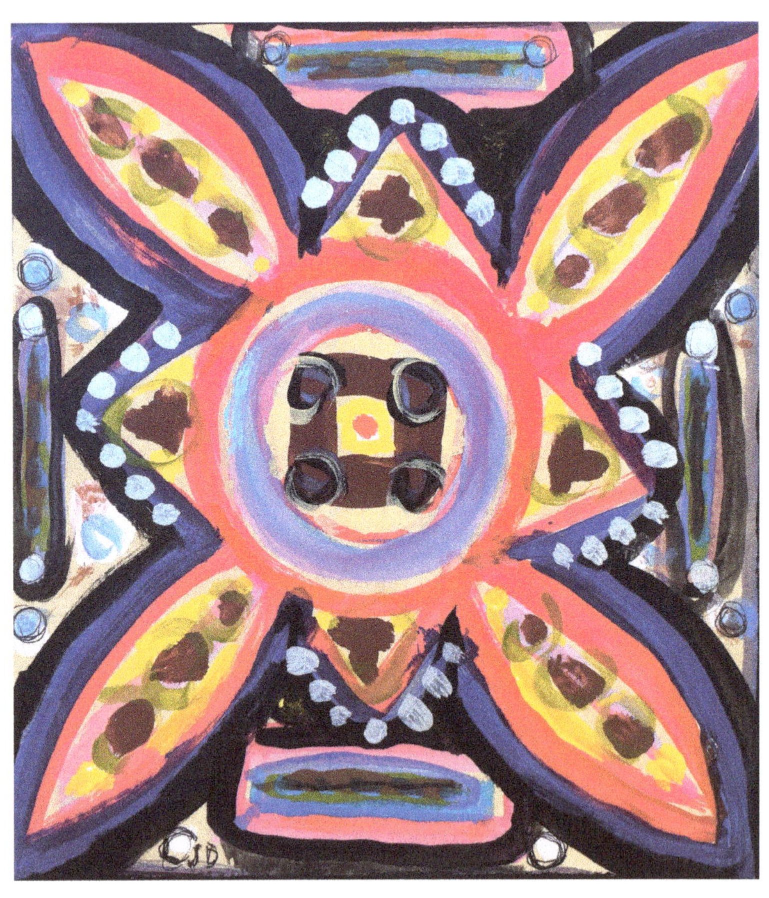

Four Truths for Life

Suffering is a Given

Life contains suffering; this we all know;
Pain and misery all around us we can clearly show.
This situation we need to accept and understand,
Otherwise in our life on shaky ground we'll stand!

Suffering comes from loss and impermanence.
But there's also the inherent suffering of existence,
Including the pain of birth, sickness, old age, and death.
All these things and more are found in life's breadth.

Reasons for Suffering

Nothing happens without a cause;
This should make us deeply pause.
It applies to all the misery we'd like to flee.
The origin of suffering, therefore, we need to see.

We foolishly sow, and then a painful harvest reap;
Such cause and effect will us in suffering definitely keep!
We vent destructive emotions without thought,
In other habits and tendencies also we get caught!

Decreasing Suffering

So, if there are causes for living life with dissatisfaction,
There must also be causes that will bring about its cessation.
Some of the causes of pain can be pacified,
Through which the easing of suffering is implied.

Our destructive emotions and habits can be subjugated,
And fewer erroneous perceptions and concepts fabricated!
This will bring a measure of peace and contentment;
And enable life lived without undue anger or resentment.

A Path to Consider

To reduce suffering, a spiritual journey is needed;
An effective path exists that many have heeded.
For our lives, this path presents eight parts;
Over time, they've enlightened human hearts.

We start with a realistic *view* and correct *intention*;
Then we also need wholesome *speech* and right *action*.
Essential too are a good *livelihood* and *determination*;
Finally, the practice of *mindfulness* and *meditation*.

This path is timeless and universal in nature;
It transcends peoples, history, and culture.
It will help greatly on your life's way,
With a sound perspective of suffering day-to-day.

By ourselves we can only do so much,
From a Higher Power we do need a touch.
We need help and soul transformation
So we can transcend this earthly misformation.

This will yield true deliverance, peace, and perfection;
A state of untold joy, beauty, and indeed glorification.

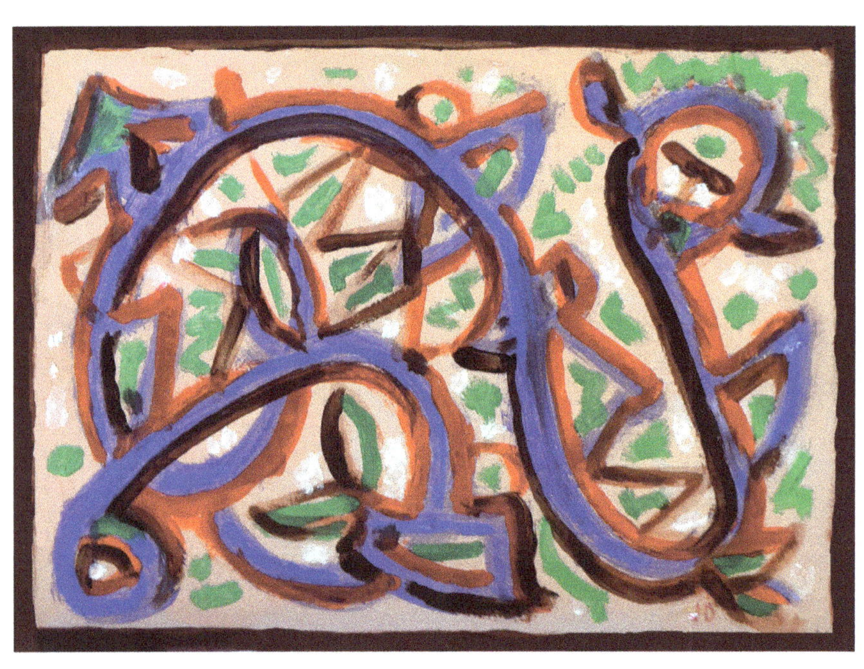

Ups and Downs in Life

Life always has its ups and downs,
Which may at first cause us frowns.
To expect life to be otherwise,
In reality, is not very wise.

To hope for only pleas*ure* is unrealistic,
In this earthly life, that's far too optimistic!
Never wanting to suffer is a wrong view to maintain.
It is a normal part of life to have some *pain*.

We're happy whenever we *gain* and get more;
But it's another story when some *loss* we score!
To only want gain, and never loss, is not realistic;
For this earthly life, it's ignorantly idealistic!

How we're pleased and rejoice, when some *fame* we get,
Yet, may feel crushed when by feelings of *insignificance* we're met!
To only desire and yearn for status and position,
In the here and now, is not a true-to-life condition!

So wonderful we feel when from others *praise* we get,
Yet, when *blame* comes our way, we quickly get upset!
To only want to be well thought of, by one and all,
In our life, is under a serious delusion to fall!

To embrace these eight worldly concerns by you and me,
Is *not* the way to live a life that is truly free!
Both *attachment* and *aversion* will leave us in suffering trapped!
There's a better, middle way, that indeed for us has been mapped.

That way is to *accept* life as it emerges, we're told,
With open heart and mind allow reality before us unfold.
Difficult as it can be, by accepting come what may,
We will find a great, more peaceful, middle way.

Countless complex causes and conditions are at play,
That make it impossible for all things to go our way.
But, to continually fear any form of pain,
Doesn't benefit life in the physical domain.

Ups and downs in life will no doubt arrive,
And we'll have to do the best we can to survive.
May we take what comes in our stride,
Accepting what we encounter – and thrive!

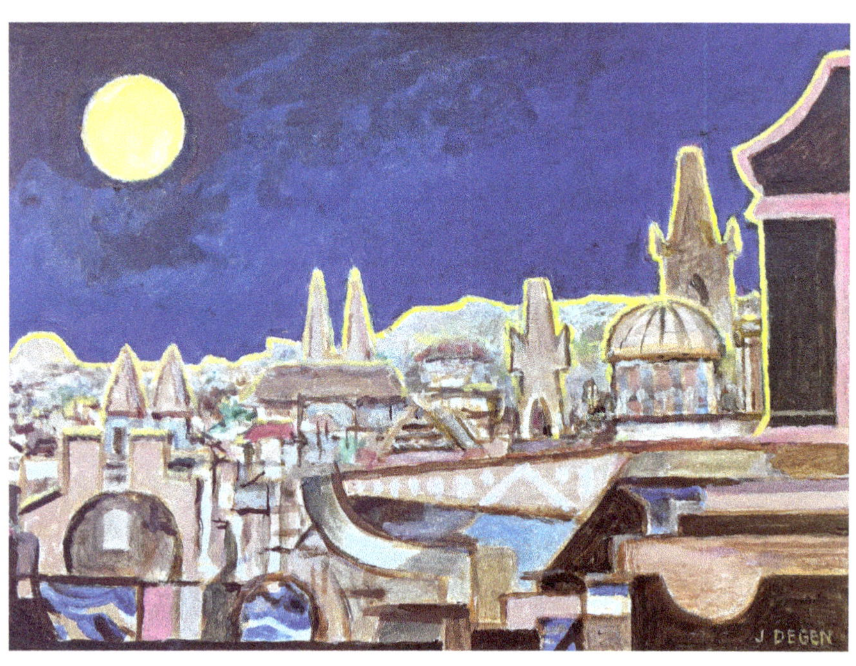

J DEGEN

Toward a Future of Well-Being

The universe has laws that are simple but profound;
When reflected upon deeply, they may even astound.
Our *wholesome* deeds will happiness ultimately bring;
While *unwholesome* actions will in the end result in suffering.

We reap what we sow, as we may well know;
Though in our life, it doesn't always seem so.
The harvest comes after some time, not right away;
And also in life there are more complex rules at play.

Avoiding ten kinds of acts, in three groups, can us instruct:
Physical acts: killing, stealing, and sexual misconduct;
Verbal acts: lying, discord, harsh words, and idle chatter;
Mental acts: coveting, ill will, wrong views – all these matter.

May we not the life of any living being unnecessarily take;
Distinctions of "big" or "small" when it comes to life we cannot make.
Instead of killing, may we seek to protect and save lives;
To not hurt, but help; and to be one who for pro-life strives!

May we not another's property take if not offered.
Deprivation by force, stealth, or deceit, many have suffered.
Instead of stealing, may we give as we are able,
Generously and from the heart, share from our table.

May we avoid sexual misconduct which can take various forms,
All of which violate pure conduct and healthy social norms.
Instead, may we be moral and escape any serious character blot.
Moral behaviour is important whether anyone is watching or not.

May we not consciously lie and say what is not true;
Nor deceitfully twist things and speak something untrue.
Instead, may we renounce lying and every form of falsehood;
And always speak lovingly and from the heart what's good.

May we not say what divides others and promotes discord,
Separating people who get on well and are of one accord.
Instead, may we reconcile parties in disagreement,
Out of dispute, create harmony and agreement.

May we avoid harsh speech and offensive talk of any kind,
Cruelly exposing someone's faults and upsetting their mind.
Instead, may we always use pleasant and kind words,
Speaking gently and politely as opportunity affords.

May we not engage in idle gossip or useless chatter,
Including frivolous jokes and things that don't matter.
Instead, may we discuss worthwhile subjects,
Engaging in meaningful talk with positive effects.

May we not covet someone's place and possessions,
Having desirous thoughts almost to the point of obsessions.
Instead, may we be satisfied with our own good portion;
And also rejoice in others' virtues, merits, and good fortune.

May we not wish harm, malice or ill on another person,
Brooding with hate or anger; glad when for them things worsen.
Instead, may we cultivate the desire to help them,
To benefit and want their good, rather than condemn.

May we not persist in wrong or perverted views,
And with harmful beliefs and concepts our mind confuse.
Instead, may we root ourselves in what is authentic and true,
Holding it fast, but not denounce another's view.

Unwise and wise acts all have consequences,
Reflecting on these can help bring us to our senses.
This also raises a question to deeply ponder:
At death, does our consciousness go on yonder?

If so, then this becomes a real game-changer for living,
Since today's deeds will future results still to us be giving!
The effects of our conduct affect not just our present life,
But will continue to bear fruit even in the afterlife!

And so, if you want to know your future situation,
Look at and carefully consider your present action.
Those who have lived well in this life will rejoice in the next;
While doers of wrong will be tormented in a woeful state and vexed.

In the long term, wholesome acts will mean a better life tomorrow,
While unwholesome actions bring suffering, pain and sorrow.
And so, wherever the mystery of life after death will take us,
Wholesome living will in the end a better future make us.

There's yet a bit more to the story –
A path that leads to future glory.
Help is available to one and all,
Who on God decide to call.

Ask for God's grace, pardon and Love Divine,
Which transforms from within and makes you fine.
This way minimises the harvest of bad seeds,
And helps you pursue loving deeds.

Its truly special and best feature
Is making of you a new creature.
A true child of God you will become,
Then be in Celestial Realms welcome.

When you have been born again,
Or, born from above, we could say,
Your promised future inheritance is great.
So ask for God's Love – no need to wait!

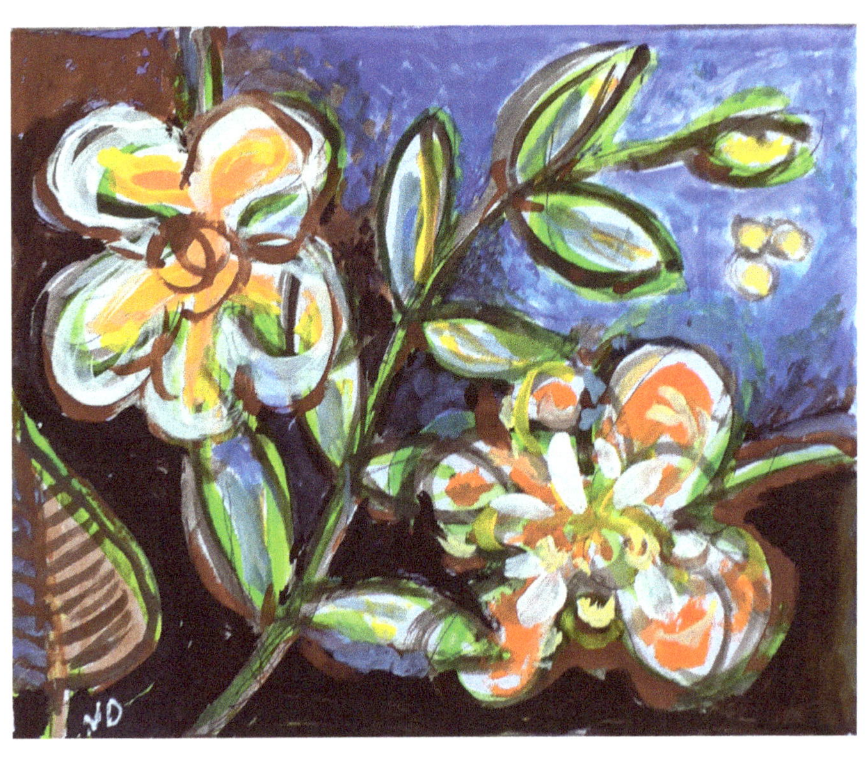

Cherish the Present Moment

How precious are times with friends, even moments that seem plain;
For, once gone, they can never be experienced again!

So, we need to savour and treasure our times with people;
Using each moment to edify, for there may be no sequel.

All phenomena come from causes and conditions in constant change,
Like a rainbow that appears when sunlight hits a shower on a range.

Occurrences influence each other in a constant dynamic,
And nothing just happens in life's events, so panoramic!

The myriad causes and conditions that brought about a situation,
Can never be recreated in just that exact formation!

One unknown day, we will each leave this life totally alone;
Nothing we can take with us from all that we presently own

Our family and friends, too, will all have to go their separate ways;
So, while we have this precious life, let's seek to live fruitful days.

There's a vital lesson and earnest advice in the lines above:
May each of our encounters be filled with heartfelt love.

Love is patient, not self-seeking, and is always kind;
It doesn't boast or envy; nor puts others in a bind.

Love is not proud and doesn't dishonour others,
No record of wrongs it keeps, but hurts and wounds it covers.

Love delights not in evil, but rejoices in the truth.
Love never fails – in one's old age, adulthood, and youth.

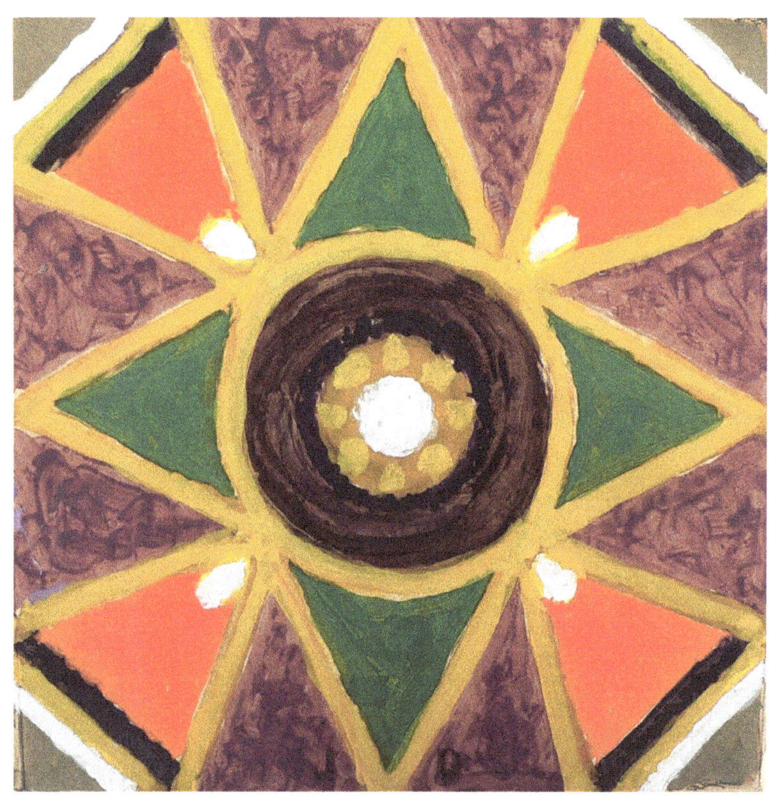

Christmastime – Something to Celebrate

Every Christmas, I see a great deal of goodwill and cheer.
I love the warmth and giving, from both afar and near.

In World War I, at Christmas, soldiers stopped fighting each other,
And for a little celebration and football game did they briefly gather.

Doesn't this show, that within our hearts lies a basic goodness?
Expressed in acts of gentleness, tenderness, and kindness.

This goodness may be obscured, as with clouds of darkness;
Often we only see, and focus on, each other's badness.

In the stiller times of this season, may we take a moment
To recognize the basic goodness in us, our endowment!

This goodness expresses itself in the desire to be happy;
The longing not to suffer that makes us so unhappy.

This innate goodness is shared by every human being;
From it springs the love and compassion that at Christmas we are
seeing!

To discover this goodness within is a key to life's fulfilment;
It's indeed an insight and understanding that is very potent.

It avoids the needless torment of seeing another as the opponent;
Instead, we'll see a oneness, with all humans an at-one-ment!

As we deeply ponder this truth, we touch on one of life's mysteries;
In all the stresses of life, this is something that not everybody sees.

So, as we enjoy the friendly attitudes at this time of year;
Isn't a basic, universal goodness displayed before us here?

To me, the smiles, sharing with the needy, the love at Christmas,
Shows the good heart within us – oh, let me not dismiss this!

May you have the best Christmas you've ever had with friends and kin;
And, where you, too, may discover the treasure buried within!

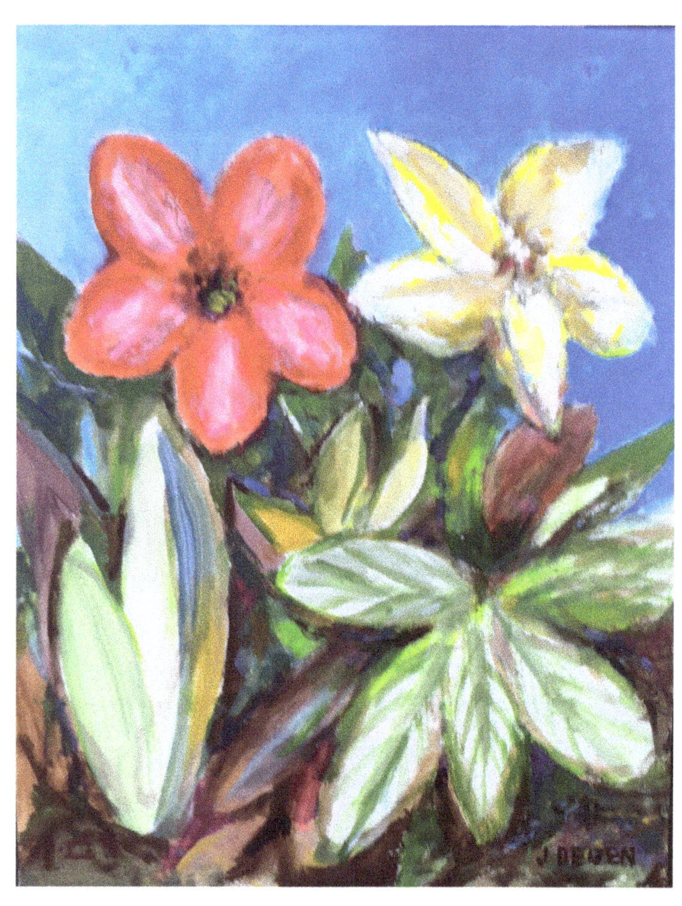
J BEWEN

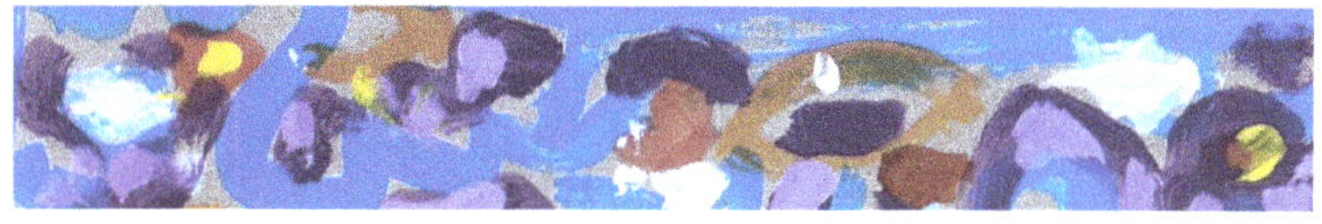

Acceptance

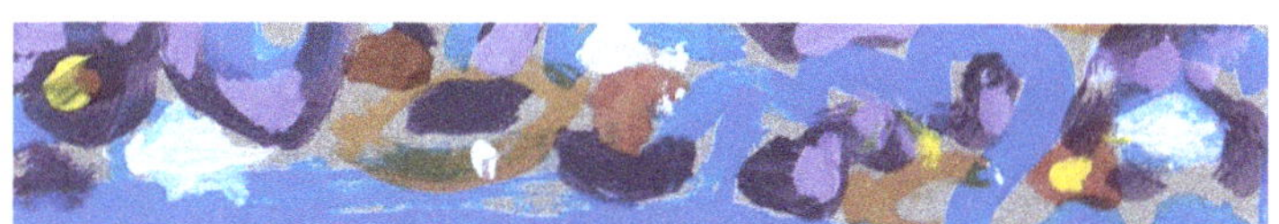

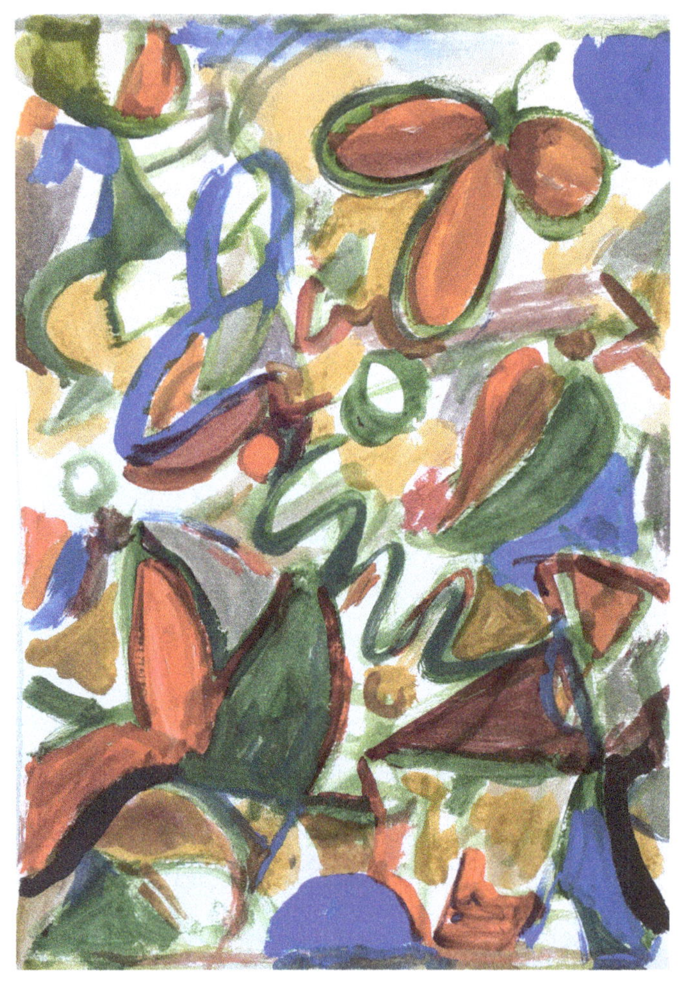

Accepting Others

Living with other people in this wondrous and interdependent existence,
We need to accept one and all as they are – without resistance.

Allowing – giving fellow humans freedom and joy to be themselves,
Not projecting expectations and judgments on them from ourselves.

Cherishing – loving care for others equal to self-cherishing,
Showing them only kindness, and never be disparaging!

Compassion – fostering other persons' welfare and well-being,
Deeply desiring to alleviate their burdens, pain or suffering.

Equanimity – seeking to free oneself of attachment and aversion,
And showing goodwill equally to all, not casting any aspersion.

Patience – forbearing difficult situations with people,
And not reacting with anger or being somehow deceitful.

Thankfulness – being grateful for our precious human existence,
And always willing to render, as we can, to others heartfelt assistance.

These qualities of goodwill, used with discernment and wisdom,
Help free the heart and mind from sorrow and suffering's prison.

May all find happiness and cultivate the causes of happiness,
And alleviate this life's sorrow by seeking to avoid its causes.

May all come to find supreme joy beyond all sorrow;
And free from greed and hate live in a better tomorrow.

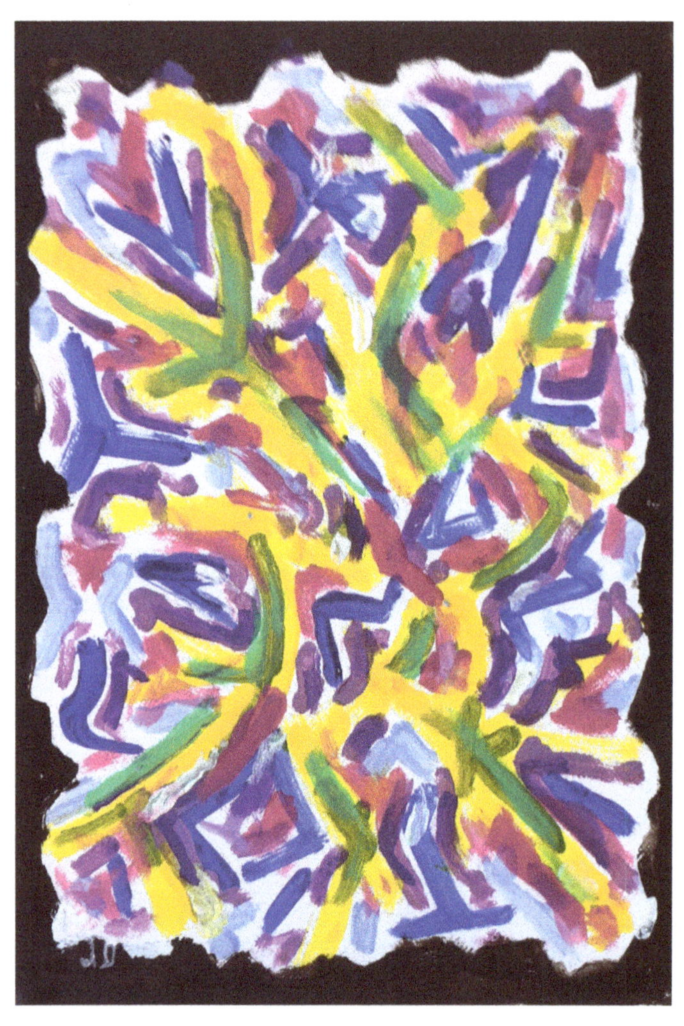

Accepting Life's Circumstances

Part I

Together we're partakers in this mystery called life,
With laughter and tears, joys and sorrows, it is rife!

Day by day, reality unrolls in fresh, unexpected ways.
At times it delights us; at other times, it us dismays!

If we can make room for and *allow reality to unfold*,
More joy we'll feel, as well as peace of mind behold.

If we can let go and *cease our desire for continual control*,
An innate wisdom, love and compassion will begin us console.

If we can *cast aside our tendency to grasp or to push away*,
Profound insights will emerge and a role in our life start to play.

If we can *empty out or put away our ego-driven agenda*,
Then, to reality as it emerges, we'll better be able to surrender.

If we can *practice an open heart and mind to whatever may come*,
Receiving what life brings will lead to a more peaceable outcome.

If we can *take responsibility and courageously do what we can*,
We'll be able to accept with serenity the things we can't do or plan.

Part II

To accept reality as it unwraps before our eyes,
Is something to which we can all aspire and rise.

Answers we want, but do not always receive,
As much as we'd like to know the whys and then to them cleave.

Calmness we need to take what may unexpectedly come;
To do what we can, but accept what we cannot overcome.

Changes in life we have to reckon with all the time,
Since they an unstoppable aspect are of our life-time.

Expectations and hopes we all have and hold onto much,
But they may not come to pass the way we wish as such.

Patience we need with what arises and develops day to day;
As life brings what we don't envisage or want to come our way.

Thankfulness we need, and to see we are part of a vast, sacred reality,
That the cosmos is permeated with love that never ceases in actuality!

May this transforming love by as many as possible be discovered;
It is so near and close to each of us, lying ready to be uncovered!

May this love help each of us in the here and now live a better life,
And avoid reaping the painful effects of wrong actions in the after-life.

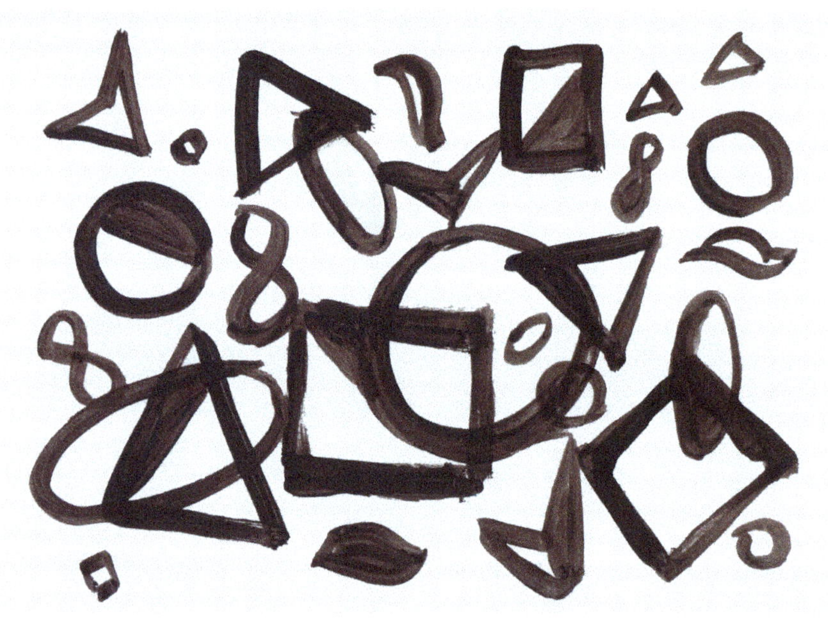

Unexpected News

Over lunch I heard my dear wife say,
"Lawrence did have a stroke yesterday."

My heart felt grief by this unexpected news from afar.
We never know what can happen that our lives will jar!

As has been seen, death doesn't wait to see,
What still needs to be done by you and me.

We can so easily have the illusion of believing,
That we have much life ahead of us, which is deceiving.

Isn't life like a dream that can be interrupted at any time?
And so, taking care of what is truly essential is prime!

The thought of death need not be morbid and depressing;
Rather, it can be motivation to do what is really pressing!

Some say, "Let me later on give thought to life's end";
Yet death is unpredictable; on such thinking we can't depend!

Much in daily life can suddenly turn into a cause of death;
We can never know on what day we'll take our last breath!

An ancient writer said that as a river rushes to the sea,
Days and nights fly; and life flows away inexorably!

There is a right timing for everything,
Let not time to prepare for life's end be vanishing.

Death is a threshold which we have to cross alone;
May we not waste our life now, to later bitterly groan!

How marvellous the miracle of life truly is!
May we use our days now to ensure future bliss!

J.DEGEN

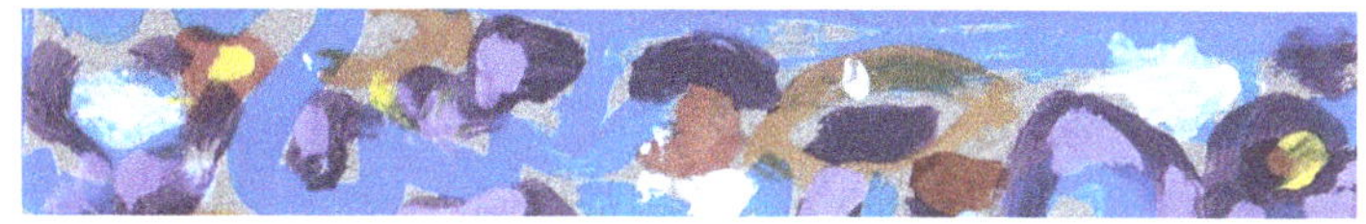

End of Life Reflections

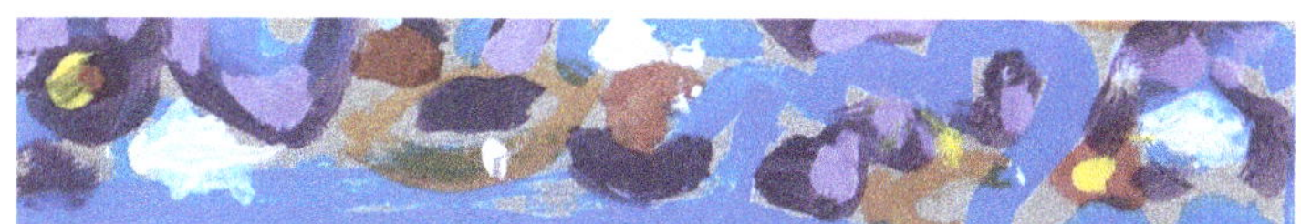

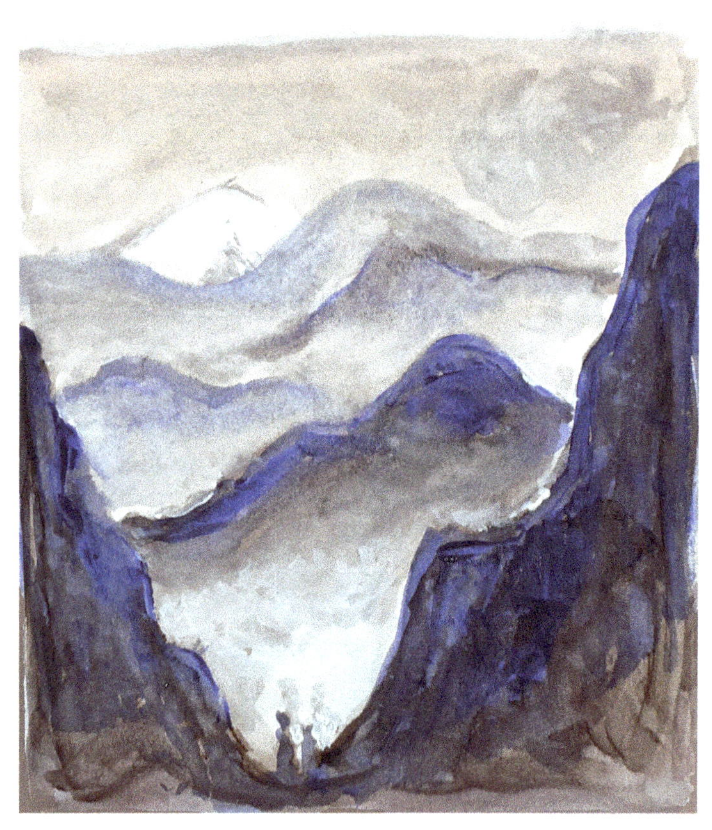

You Never Know When It's Time to Go

My mother phoned on a Thursday night;
We said good-bye on a note quite bright.
Early the next week, we received a call;
Mother had died; shocked were we all!

With dad one day, I visited his Ukrainian friend;
On parting, good will and cheer to us he did send.
Two weeks later, he died resting after lunch one afternoon;
It was so unexpected, and after our visit far too soon!

Lloyd taught English with us in Hradec from the start;
His students all much loved him truly from their heart.
As I recall, Lloyd, when he was only sixty-two,
During a bad winter was conquered by the flu!

My wife's mum we saw in her home in Cleveland;
Nice things we did while here from a distant land.
Then, shockingly, she died in her sleep one February night;
It left us sad and sobered to reflect on her plight.

Kathy loved her mountain home after teaching overseas;
She kept in touch from her scenic place in the high Rockies.
We were stunned one day to get news from her friend:
A brain aneurysm brought her life to an unexpected end!

Mary planned a stay in Prague looking so inviting;
To spend time with former friends all sounded exciting.
Not long after, we had heard that Mary became ill;
And then she died so quickly; a big shock it is still!

Mike, a youth leader, was loved by young and old;
All liked hearing the great tales that often he had told.
Cycling home from a camp late one summer day,
Mike suffered a heart attack and died along the way.

There is a crucial lesson in the sober verses above:
May each of our good-byes be filled with heartfelt love.
We never know when a loved one for the last time we'll see,
Always, therefore, it is vital to part in harmony.

Death will come to one and all, that we know for sure;
But, know we cannot, when it will knock at our door.
So be careful with the selfish plans you make,
Neglecting important tasks you need to undertake!

Hence, as much as possible, striving to be ready,
Try to always make your life fruitful and not heady.
The truth is that you'll never know
When it's time for you to go!

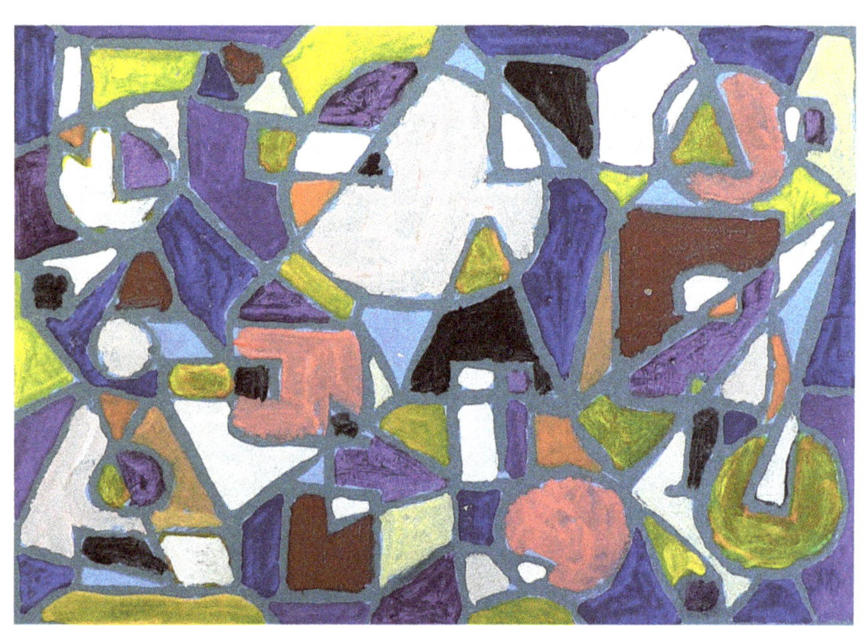

Untimely Departure

After making our payment at a local carpet shop,
The owner mentioned something that quickly made us stop!

"My son's friend died in a car crash yesterday sometime;
He was just seventeen; what tragedy before Christmastime."

The words caused us to pause – they were like fiery darts;
Time stood still for a moment, as they sank into our hearts.

Touched by this painful news, I couldn't help but ponder;
Much in life remains a mystery, so much for us to wonder.

What's there to learn from this young man's untimely passing?
Can we find in his death some deep lessons long-lasting?

Our world is a complex web of multiple causes and conditions;
No-one, young or old, can be sure to fulfil all their ambitions.

Once we visited a nearby cemetery in a quiet bushland setting;
The sobering lesson learnt that day, too, is worth not forgetting.

Tombstones we saw for infants, children and young people,
Adults in their prime, and seniors – all in their graves lay equal!

No one is exempt from the impermanence of life;
Age isn't a deciding factor for Death's ubiquitous knife.

We may in our minds accept that death is a certain reality for all,
But this tragic demise and graveyard visit pierced our heart's wall!

May this insight that our length of life is uncertain,
Spur us on to not spend our time here in vain!

Life can cease at any age, taking that last breath;
No one knows the exact time and causes of their death.

May the tragic news that we learned that afternoon,
Help others grasp life's realities, and so for many be a boon!

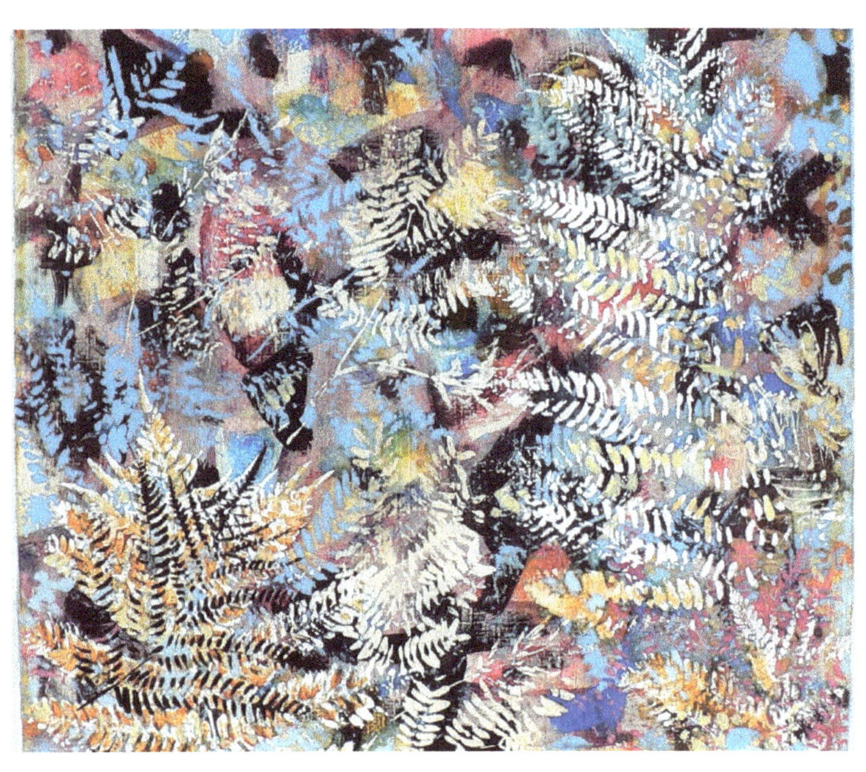

Before It's Too Late

She sat before us in deep depression and despair;
At ninety, her life became an endless frustrating care.

Onset of diabetes had been one concern for her,
And she couldn't see clearly, but rather in a blur.

Walking was hard, and her hands were now shaking.
She felt so bad – all seemed like trouble in the making.

Softly she said that she wanted to end her life –
To exit from what now was just frustration and strife.

She hoped a sleeping pills overdose would do it painlessly;
But, if not, she was ready to slit her wrists courageously.

My wife and I listened in silence, stunned by her words of pain.
She felt as if down in a black abyss, never to see light again.

Gently we asked if she had any belief in a Higher Power;
A brief prayer she uttered, but without hope for this grave hour.

The visit became deadly serious and with danger smitten,
When the lady showed us two suicide notes she had written!

We left her apartment that Christmas Eve, deep in thought;
Right away informing professionals, doing what we ought.

This despairing lady had had a good, well-to-do life on the whole.
But, now in time of urgent need, she had no anchor for her soul.

Storms of life assail us all, be it tragedy, illness, or losses of old age.
But building faith may be impossible when life's winds around us rage!

May we see the golden chance to get ready that now exists,
To prepare for our final days, and unforeseen life twists.

Now is the time to turn our life in the right direction,
Starting with heartfelt introspection and deep reflection.

Deep within is a basic goodness shared by every human being;
From it springs love and compassion that at times we can't help seeing!

True, this goodness may be obscured, as with clouds of darkness;
Never noticed when we only focus on the surrounding harshness.

As life goes on, may we nurture more of our innate goodness,
Seeing in our heart hidden wisdom, peace, joy, and pureness!

While still young, it isn't too early to prepare for the future now,
As no one can prevent, nor insure against, an untimely "ciao"!

Even if old and frail, until our last breath, it isn't too late to change
The course of our life, though this at first may come across as strange!

Some may be anxious what awaits them after they die;
Yet, this needn't be a time to be frightened, or in helplessness to sigh.

May we each take time daily, while there is a "today",
To build an anchor for our life that will hold us, come what may!

In this effort, we can follow whatever spiritual path we wish,
So that we are prepared for life's end and all that life may us dish.

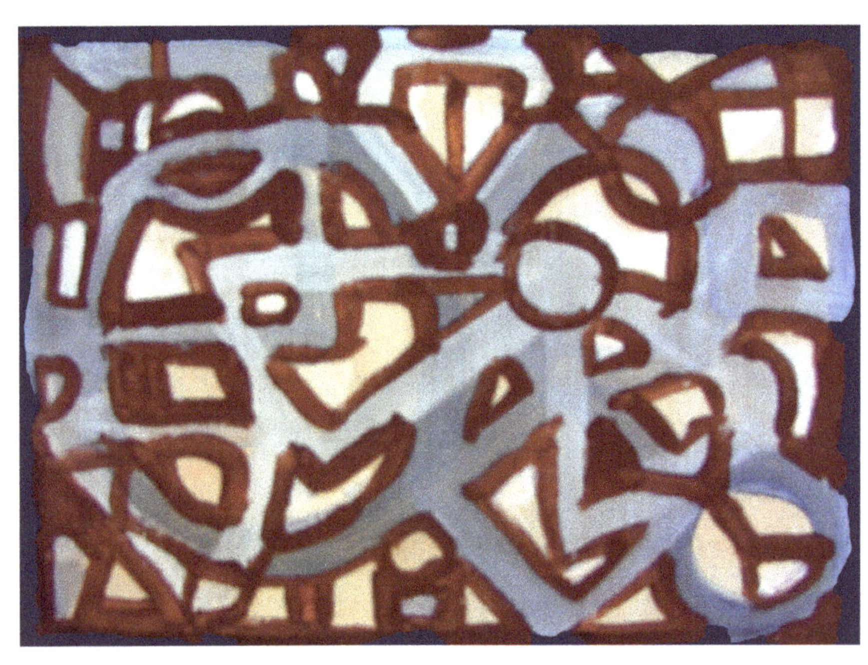

Saying Goodbye

Before I go, I must thank you from my heart,
For all your love and kindness from the start.

Those wonderful years we have shared and been glad,
They can never be re-lived and in the same way had.

Each moment in a day is unique and precious,
So, let's be very grateful, and always gracious.

Though through death we must all in due time go,
For each of us, another existence will follow.

Science suggests life is one unbroken whole.
And over our fate, we have considerable control.

The law of cause and effect is always working in time and space;
That explains such things as why people end up in a certain place.

All our kind and loving virtuous deeds to date,
Will ripen and richly bless us in our future state.

Here words are now added based on a Jim Reeves' song.
They fit the theme of life's end, and yet remaining strong.

A time comes for each one to say, "Adios amigo, adios dear friend".
The road we have travelled together is coming to an end.

We will all in endless time and space our future spend.
But for now on earth, a time comes to say, "Adios my dear friend".

Adios wonderful companion, may we shed no needless tears;
May your mañanas bring joy and peace, without pointless fears.

Bravely may we say, "Adios kind companion, what must be must be".
In the end, we each have to journey to our own chosen destiny.

This short life with its joys and tears can't be our whole story!
Isn't there, beyond Mother Earth, a sphere of awesome glory?

Surely we're more than this limited body in which we abide.
In fact, our mind/soul goes on after the body has died.

Birth and death are only sacred doors through which we pass.
But, for now, we just see this as if through a murky glass.

If life goes on, then we will meet again in a new tomorrow.
This hope fanned into flame reduces goodbye's sorrow

So, my dear friend, take good care of yourself today;
Always reflect on what's vital in life along the way.

Past this life, surely we'll all go on, time in another realm to spend;
Hence, when our time comes, may we bravely face this life's end.

May we say with hope, faith and love, "Adios for now, my precious
friend";
Awaiting the time we meet again, and life's mysteries better
comprehend!

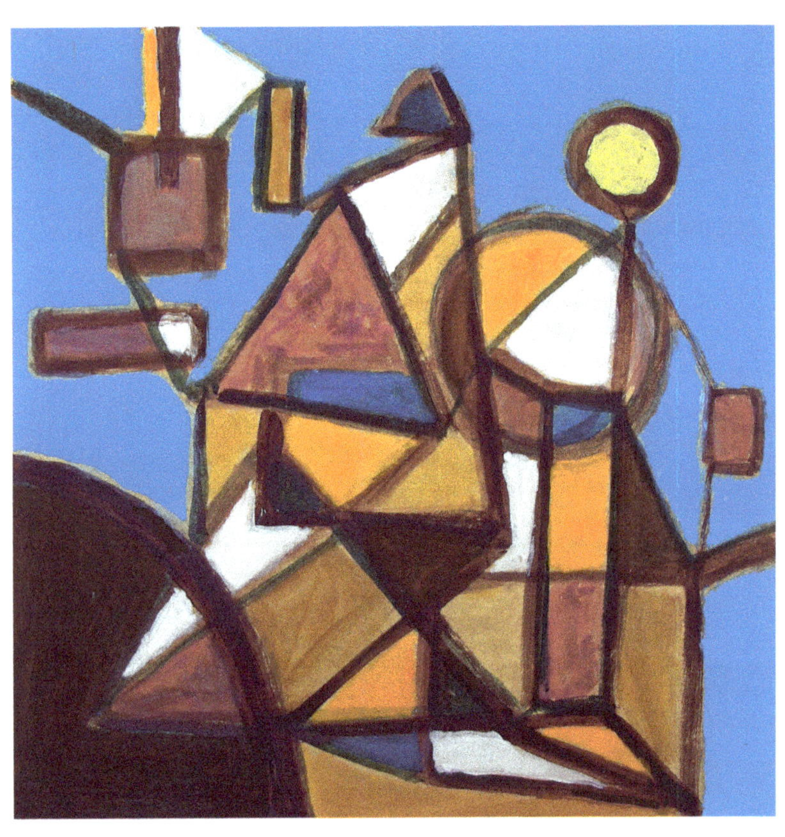

Uncle Bill

As a child, I used to visit uncle Bill,
Living in the country with aunt Jill.
Around their property with my cousins I would run,
Playing with their animals was great fun.

When I began a job, I got out of touch,
And didn't see my uncle and aunt very much.
I was busy and time was tight,
But from time to time I would briefly write.

I used to ask, "How's uncle Bill?"
An answer came, written by aunt Jill:
"Uncle Bill is still around,
Slowing down, but in mind sound."

While thinking on my childhood past,
Recently I again asked:
"How's uncle Bill,
Is he with us still?"

The answer, in shaky writing, came:
"It is no longer the same.
I'm very sorry to have to say,
Uncle Bill passed away yesterday."

Suddenly it dawned on me,
As I quietly sipped green tea:
I, too, will go uncle Bill's way,
I'm afraid to admit and say!

Therefore, let me make the most of today,
Before like a bird in a tree, I will fly away!
Let me find out what this life is all about,
And how to ensure a smooth and happy flight!

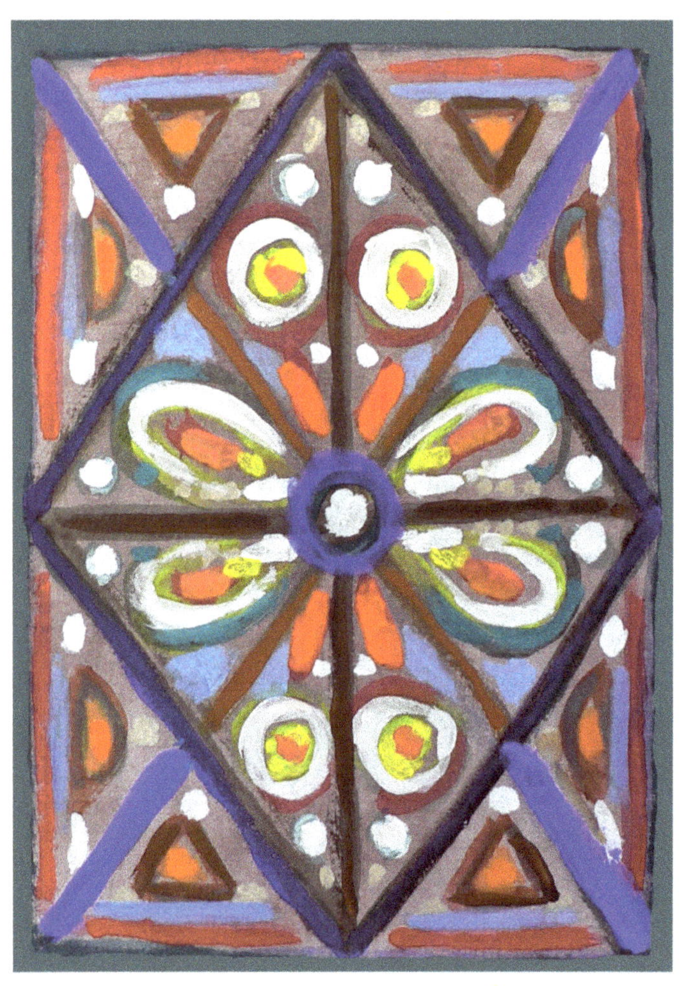

Reflection on Old Age

Maria confided to my wife and me, "I wish I were dead; oh, my . . .",
We listened as she shared her suffering, with an inward sigh.

An eventful life with her now dead husband, she could look back to.
Born in Vienna, she had escaped from the aftermath of World War II.

Sitting in her luxury flat, in a prestigious retirement village,
Surrounded by quality items, we reflected on her privilege.

From her balcony, she had a panoramic view to the sea,
Yet, now at ninety, she had become terribly lonely.

Her health had been worsening, beginning with a bad fall,
Then a light stroke; and, now the onset of diabetes wasn't all.

She realized that her mind was starting to fail her;
Her memory now poor; and, at times, her vision a blur.

She had purchased a quality motor scooter for mobility;
But, with dizzy spells, her doctor advised against its suitability.

As we talked and reflected in the quiet afternoon, with tea and croissant,
She looked around her living room and said, "Take whatever you want".

"I can no longer enjoy them, and have no further need for any of this."
Silence ensued; lost in a moment of thought, I began to reminisce:

Memories came back of another immigrant, Mario, who became wealthy;
Real estate at a low price he purchased when he was young and healthy.

Land prices went up, and when he sold his land, he "made a mint"!
He had a dream home built in a nice part of town; no small stint!

We'll never forget him, sitting lonely outside his mansion.
"Bugger the house!", he exclaimed, full of deep-felt frustration.

How the suffering of old age can be for some a terrible plight,
And further aggravated without a higher vision or insight.

We don't all have to end up unhappy and weary of life like this;
True though, with uncertainty of what may happen, it may not be bliss.

Yet, to prevent bleak and despairing latter days from overtaking us,
Let's now use wisely each day and hour, and see their beauty thus.

May we seek a higher purpose and noble values in this life,
Being grateful for everything, and daily living without strife.

While we are able, may we toward others be generous and kind;
Looking back on life with no regrets, and with deep peace of mind.

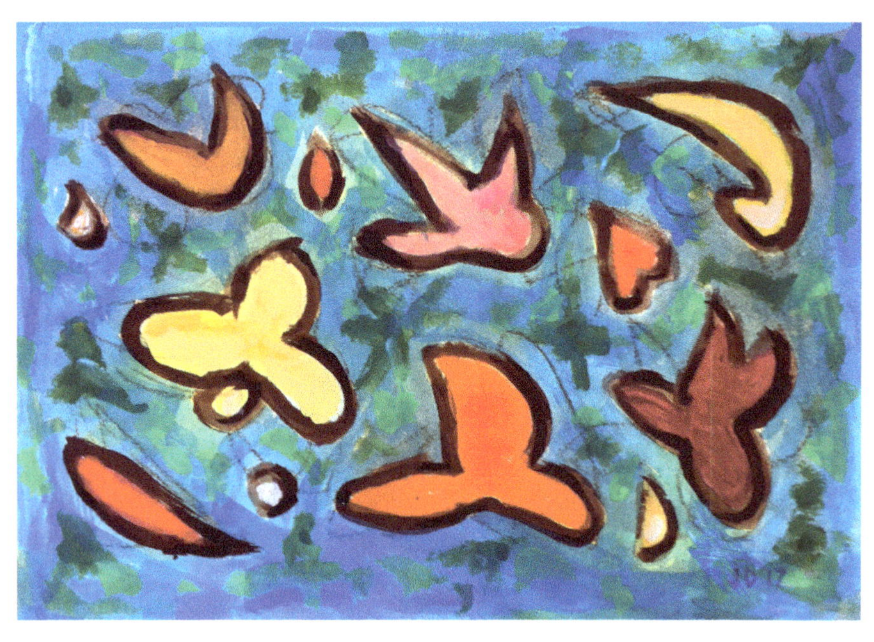

Airport Departure Reflections

On a cloudless winter morning, my wife boarded the airport bus,
Embarking on an overseas trip, she waved goodbye to us.

After the hustle and bustle of final activity,
The stillness and loneliness now hit home to me.

Closing the door, I went to my study and sat in solitude.
Sipping a cup of tea, I paused, in a deeply reflective mood.

All my wife took with her was her handbag and small suitcase;
All else was left behind: family, friends, possessions, and place.

Isn't this reminiscent of what each of us faces at death,
When the time comes for our body to exhale its last breath?

As the body and soul separate, everything will be left behind;
All with which we were so closely for our whole life aligned.

We will each journey into a new cosmic realm alone;
Leaving on earth our family, friends, money, and all else that we own!

I look around the room and ask: Why all this hoarding?
What use are these old items? I feel an inner warning.

My wife had well planned and prepared for her trip abroad;
Have I the reality of my future journey to a new realm ignored?

She met with success and joy throughout her trip;
In her good preparation for it, she had let nothing slip.

How earnestly am I preparing for my future reward?
Ignoring the law of cause and effect I really cannot afford!

Our present life is like a story, produced by our deeds in the past;
Our future life is the story we're now writing by our actions cast!

May we each create a magnificent story,
Not one that will be a sorrowful history.

The world is like a stage where everyone plays a part;
Our deeds daily script our role; this we must take to heart!

Once our script is written, there's truth in the "Que Sera, Sera" song;
"Whatever will be, will be"; and so, may we not script what is wrong!

In an ancient writing from the long distant past,
We have these thoughts that will never us outlast:

Suffering here and beyond, the wrongdoers hurt in both.
They are stricken, seeing the pain of which they are loathe!

Delighting here and beyond, the well doers rejoice in each world.
They celebrate, seeing the virtues of their good actions unfurled!

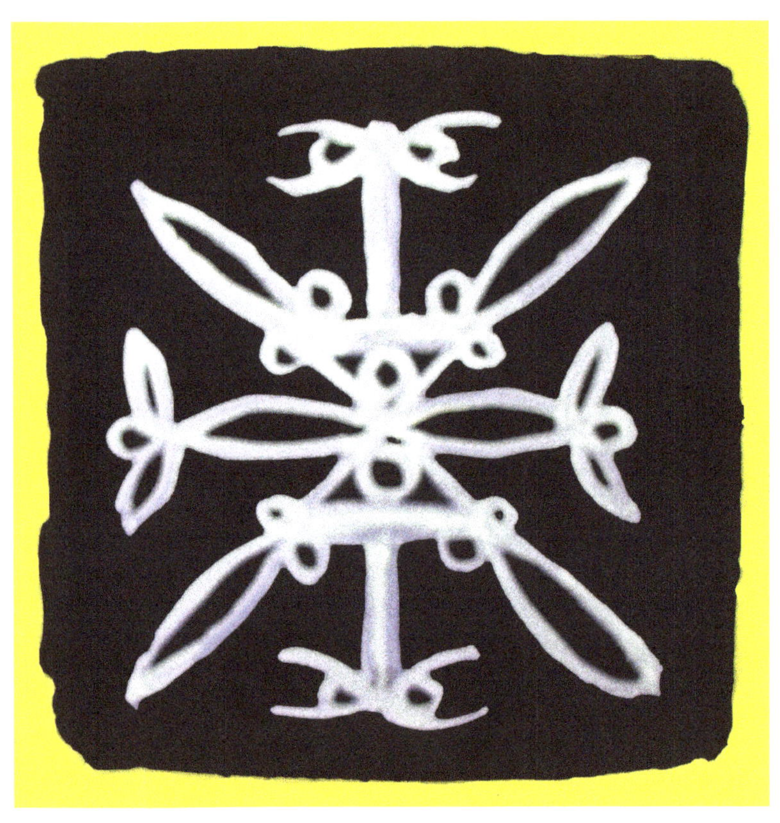

Dying Friend

I'm thinking of my dying friend,
In hospital, facing his life's end.
He's lost much of his mental clarity,
And is plagued by physical disability.

His home, to him once dear,
Is now no longer near.
The prognosis is a long hospital stay;
This could lead to his great dismay.

Such reflections lead to a vital question:
What's most important in my life's direction?
Is this life, with its joys and sorrows, all there is?
Or, could there be, beyond this, a realm of bliss?

Or, is something else after death us awaiting?
A fate we bring about that might be devastating?
Are there effects of our earthly actions,
Consequences of our here-and-now reactions?

Scientists now see reality as an unbroken wholeness;
"Life" and "death" are only aspects of a oneness.
"Death" is part of an endless movement or flow;
Consciousness or soul go on, this we may know.

And so, the results of today's actions carry over.
Death isn't a state of nothingness, we'll discover.
Consequences of our past actions follow us after we die,
Like an ever-present shadow, seen clearly by the eye.

In this life, we can see how cause and effect operate;
That pattern, however, is not always linear and straight.
Yet, overall, virtue and good deeds will happiness bring,
And negativity and vices will result in suffering.

In the next life, all our loving deeds from the past,
Will bring joy and well-being that may be vast!
Also, negative actions will result in suffering,
That we'll find ourselves proportionally enduring.

Such reflections many have yet to earnestly face.
May we each do so while we have time and space.
We can see how our time in this life quickly disappears;
May we choose what will be before our life end appears!

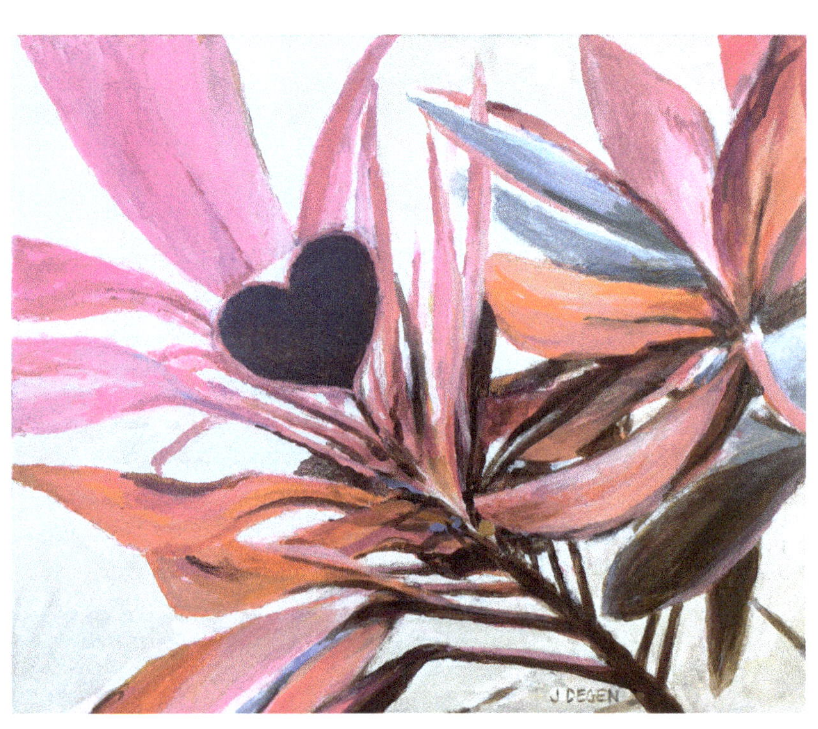
J DEGEN

For Your Remaining Life Journey

To dear Lynn, a long-time friend,
Some deeper thoughts we'd like to send.

You are kept in our heart and mind.
We never know what in life we'll find.

In looking back, we see a creation filled with love;
May you keep strong the faith in what lies above.

While the news about your health is sad,
We have a Help beyond that makes us glad.

If at all possible, keep a heart of cheer;
With your hope, in the end there'll be no need for fear.

Sooner or later a great journey you'll take,
It's a voyage we all in time must undertake.

Whether we like this sobering fact or not,
Not one of us stays forever in their earthly spot.

Our frail body we shall all leave behind,
But on will continue our spirit and mind.

Our best wishes to you and yours we send,
May it all work out for the best in the final end!

We can be certain that it will,
As long as in faith we can all be still.

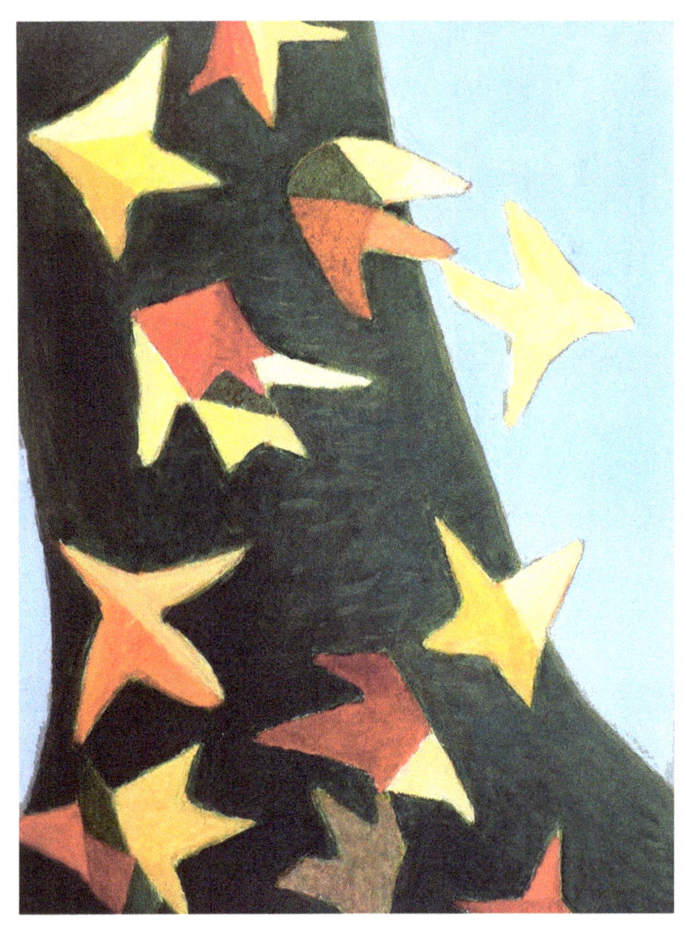

On Nearing Life's End

Wishing you a happy New Year,
Even in hard days, to find some cheer.
Luckily your family is fairly near,
So hopefully there is less to fear.

Another year! How the time does fly!
Soon we'll all leave and say good-bye.
No-one is here forever to stay,
We all know well it is that way.

When it comes the time to go,
All cares and worries just forgo.
Try to lean back and just relax,
You have lived life to the max.

All hurts and grudges put aside,
Keep your calm and peace inside.
No-one's lived a perfect life,
Without trouble and some strife.

Forgive one and forgive all,
For in this life, we all do fall.
Always keep a peaceful mind,
In your thoughts to all be kind.

Our mind's what chains or sets us free,
Care less what folk think of you or me.
Remain at peace and free from strife,
This helps to lead a happy life.

Soon an unknown trip you'll take,
It's a journey that we all must make.
Whether we like this fact or not,
None on earth stay in their spot.

Our body all we leave behind,
But on goes our soul and mind.
Keep your mind healthy and strong,
Its journey is very long.

If you've tried to do what's right,
Awaiting you is a life of delight.
If need be, there's time for change to make,
And from terror and fear give you a break.

If needed, for your wrongs feel remorse,
This would be one's duty, of course.
Then, with deep resolve and hope,
Enjoy a vision great in scope.

Look forward to your brand-new place,
Let go of any fears you face.
Keep your eyes set on what's ahead,
There'll be little for you to dread.

You'll be able to enjoy the ride,
No need for panic from your side.
Our best wishes to you we send,
It'll all work out in the end!

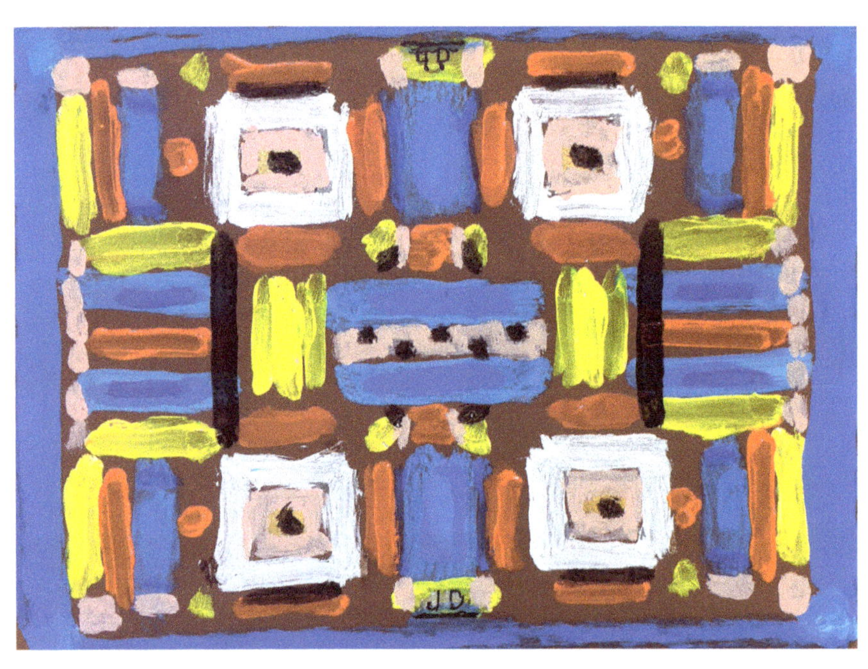

Reflections on Life and Death

He earnestly scribbled to me, 'I think I'm dying',
Moved by compassion, I almost felt like crying.
That he had had a rich and varied life, there's no doubt,
But it seemed like he struggled with what life was all about.

His heartfelt words have caused me to seriously reflect;
Well into my sixties, his comment I couldn't simply deflect.
The mindfulness of death puts everything into perspective;
Priorities it sets straight and makes us soberly reflective.

Now that the end of life has arrived at someone's door,
All their mundane concerns and pursuits are important no more.
The quest for gain, praise and pleasure no longer matters much;
We realize that everything we cling to is impermanent as such.

I thought about the many deaths that had occurred in the past;
And the uncertainty of when and how death can come, sometimes fast.
Also, the possible suffering at the time of death – especially the fear,
The separation from loved ones, friends, and all that's to us dear.

We should take time out to deeply reflect about life;
To go within and contemplate, away from the world of strife.
What is of higher value needs to be our daily focus;
And not lose our priorities in this world of hocus-pocus.

May we each come to better grasp life's deeper meaning,
Without ourselves from the world's suffering screening.
May we also remember that good and wholesome actions count,
And that these will needless problems and pain help surmount.

May everyone find a path to happiness, peace and bliss;
And life's greater design and purpose not totally miss!

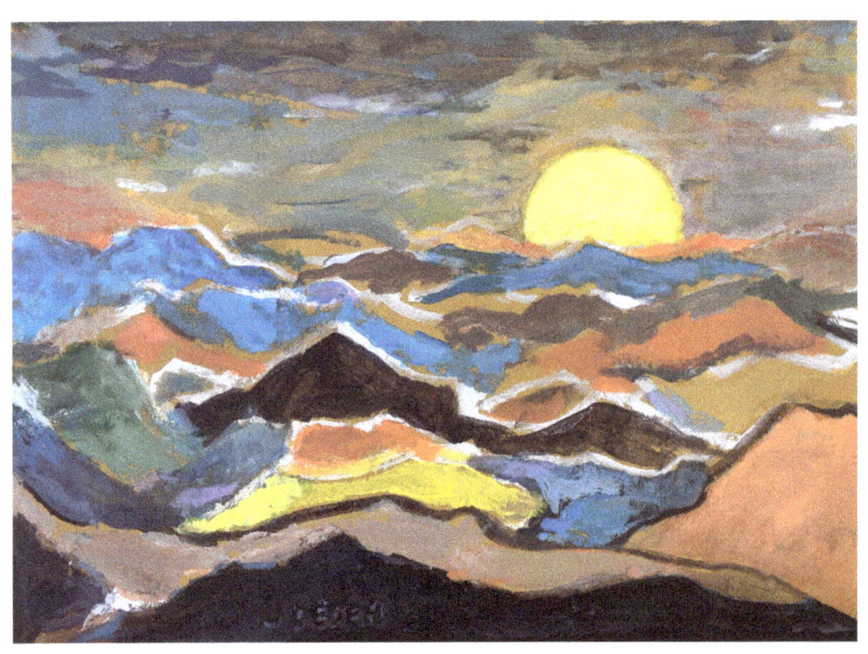

Consider the End

I write with a cloud of sadness hanging over me about a friend,
Lying in a hospital ward, terminally ill, and facing life's end.
He had had a varied and interesting life;
Lived in five states with a devoted and faithful wife.

His two children did well by the world's way of measuring success;
Though the grandchildren indulge in food and drink somewhat to
excess.
My friend could be proud of his family as far as wealth and fame;
They have made striving by the world's standards their sole aim.

A comfortable home my friend owns in a well-to-do suburb;
Now retired, lack of anything for him and his wife was almost unheard.
Proudly my friend wrote not long ago about their brand-new car;
Plans with his wife he had made for a cruise and a safari afar.

Now and then, we would sit and share a home or restaurant meal.
Yet, sadly, the conversation only with trivia or latest politics did deal.
Also, taken he was by the latest iPad or iPhone app,
So into life's rich and deeper meaning never alas did we tap.

Then, with an aggressive cancer my friend was diagnosed as such.
Yet, even with deteriorating health, his life did not change much.
He continued being fully absorbed with all of this world's affairs,
Avidly following his favourite sports teams and market shares.

Carefree weeks, months, and years had sped for him by.
The sudden news of his incurable illness truly made me sigh.
As I think of the time he had to prepare for life's final journey,
His having pursued just wealth and pleasures truly concerns me.

Many plan and live as though their earthly life will endlessly go ahead,
Not thinking how unexpectedly and quickly this existence can end instead!
In reality, there's much to take care of before we die,
Many important tasks to undertake before we see that death is nigh!

We should know what to do for ourselves even as we die;
To know what is happening; be ready to let go and say good-bye.
Above all, it's important, if at all possible, to have a peaceful death;
To have addressed our hopes and fears before taking the last breath.

Writing these stanzas, I feel sad over my friend in hospital dying,
Maybe without hope, as well as full of anguish and fear, there lying!
May we each our coming death earnestly take to heart,
And serious reflection and preparation even today start!

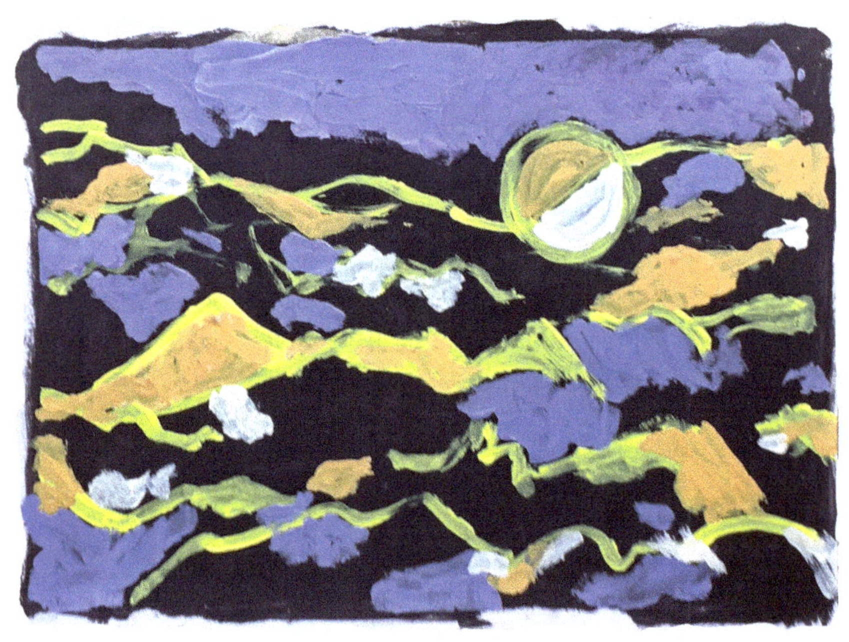

Before I Leave

While in Vienna, we stopped with an uncle at the cemetery;
At the family grave he said, "Here my wife and me they'll also bury".

He wasn't morbidly preoccupied with their mortality;
Rather, he wisely and squarely faced life's reality.

He had just retired, having turned sixty-five;
Three decades later, he peacefully died at over ninety-five.

I must pen these words while still sound in body, mind, and spirit;
Not knowing what may yet befall me, or what hardship I may inherit.

Friendship, fortune, favour – all that we have always changes;
How transient this life is – everything constantly rearranges!

Observing life, ancient sages have seen realities,
That are timeless, and by no means trivialities:

Whatever is born is impermanent and bound to die;
Whatever is stored up will in time all run dry.

Whatever comes together is bound to separate.
Whatever is built will one day collapse and abate.

So, let me share these thoughts before it is too late,
When my life's story be ended, and my next phase I await.

This journey, after we die, we must each take alone,
Without family and friends, and all that on this earth we own.

What, then, will survive and go with us beyond death?
Results of our good and evil deeds follow the last breath!

So, our urgent need in life is refuge in a trustworthy Source;
Taking to heart sacred writings, and becoming free of remorse.

While we have a chance to seek an authentic spiritual path,
May we quickly do so, and not suffer painful aftermath.

I'm very thankful for the life I've been privileged to lead,
Having had the freedom to choose what I wanted indeed!

I am most grateful for my dear parents' love and labour;
I wish them both well; may I always give them honour!

I am much indebted to Eva, my wife; and thankful for her family;
She's shown me great love; her relatives let me live happily.

Jindrich, Eva's father, deserves special attention;
It's his great kindness and respect that I must mention.

In this life, we will meet trying times, as if going through fire;
We lose what we loved, and hurt when not getting what we desire.

Painfully also, from five deadly mind poisons we cannot hide:
Ignorance, craving, hatred, as well as jealousy and pride.

Living long abroad, we were away from family and loved ones;
This affected relationships with my brothers, their daughters and sons.

Still, with many fond memories, I cherish both of my dear brothers;
And though like strangers we may be, I value their sons and daughters.

Better understanding what life is like with all its joys and pain,
Toward none, ill will, dislike, or hatred I for a moment wish to entertain.

All I have wounded through words or deeds in life's course,
This I now deeply regret, and have utmost heartfelt remorse.

I ask for forgiveness from one and all that I may have hurt inside.
The few who have injured me, it's totally forgiven from my side.

And so, farewell to each one who has shared the path of life with me,
One day I will be here with you no more; whatever will be, will be.

May I face life's end in peace, and with no fear or regrets,
And die without sadness or feeling any threats.

As we'll each in our time travel alone into that vast unknown,
May we deeply pray, so that none of us into confusion be thrown.

Finally, may we all reach our sublime potential destiny,
And one day dwell in perfect, unimagined blissful eternity!

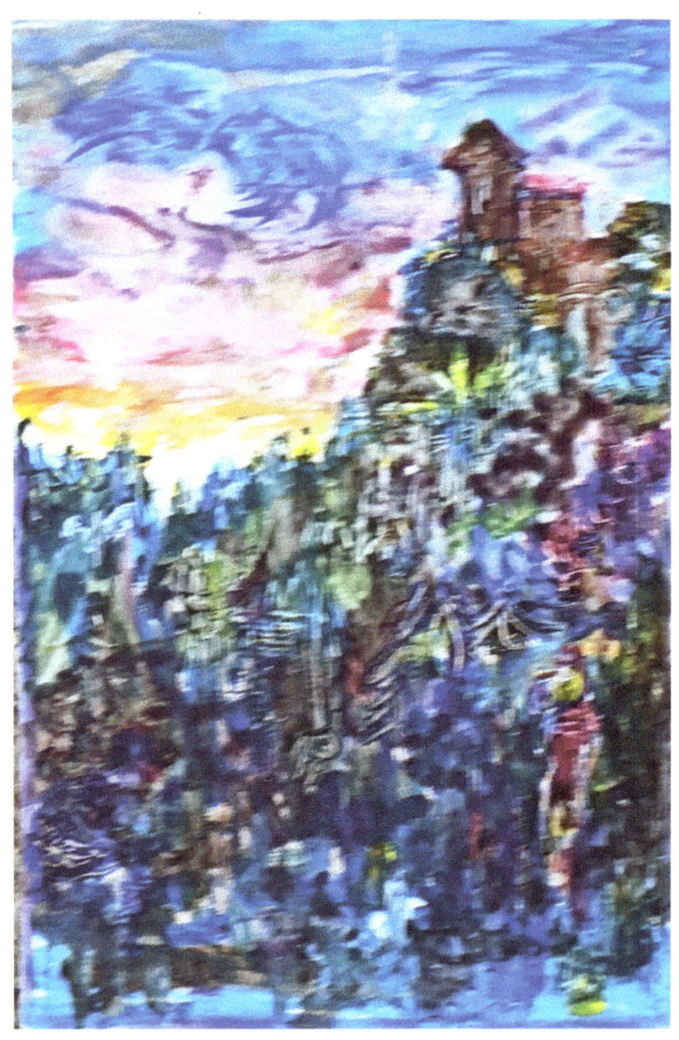

The Afterlife

Recently, we went to the funeral of a dear friend,
Who as a result of cancer had met with life's end.
At such a time as this, one cannot help but ask:
What's next? Does something survive death's mask?

Many have discussed this, some even with strife,
Whether or not there is some kind of after-life.
Plausible arguments can be presented for both sides;
Most people are unsure where the exact truth lies.

Sadly, many mistaken ideas about the after-life prevail;
But all these, once death has occurred, will be to no avail!
Some incorrectly believe that once you are dead,
Everything's finished, and there's nothing to dread.

They erroneously believe that death is a total end,
That all experience is done with, and no more time to spend.
They think there's nowhere else to go, and that's that.
It is just from dust to ashes, or to end like a gnat.

Or, that one'll be free from suffering, since nothing exists after death,
Because once one has died, all is finished with the last breath.
It is all just matter, according to scientific journal articles,
And everything can be explained as the interaction of particles.

That death may be hard to go through, many agree.
But, after it, some wrongly think, one is completely free;
As if someone picks you up and puts you in a lovely place,
With all kinds of entertainments with which to keep pace!

These people mistakenly reason that once we are dead,
To some magical realm we'll be quickly carried instead.
They do not believe that this earthly life is all that there is.
Rather, they hope to find beyond a special land of bliss.

Regrettably, these are misinformed, imagined guarantees,
Which fail to recognize and take into account basic realities!
A wishful desire to escape the true order of things,
Doesn't change anything, but rather more suffering brings.

It is a delusion to believe that there will be no suffering,
That after death, pure enjoyment all by itself up will spring.
Such thinking will only make reality more difficult to face,
When we realize too late there's no make-believe hiding-place.

It is sad that people misunderstand and carry superstitions,
About how they will live their next life in various conditions.
They don't know that their thoughts, words, and actions in this life,
Will have far-reaching consequences in their after-life.

Now, one thing we have observed, which in the profound lies:
That if someone we love reaches their end of life and dies,
Because of our love for them, it is difficult to feel and say,
That this person's totally gone and never present in any way.

We may feel that our loved ones, who have left this world behind,
Are somehow still available, and talk to them in our mind.
We like to visit the place they are buried in their remembrance.
Dreaming they're still alive, we may even see or feel their presence.

We instinctively come to believe there's an innate something,
That's not finished when we die and seem to become as nothing.
Whether we are thinking about ourselves or others,
We feel something outlives death, that nothing ever smothers.

We see ourselves not as a spent candle when the last flame goes out,
But rather as a flaming torch, a light shining all about,
As something that is transferred from one state to the next.
We pass onto another way of being, with exciting prospects!

If we can understand that death isn't nothingness or a blank state,
It doesn't become the end, nor need be something to fear or hate.
Rather, it is possible to dedicate our lives to bringing light,
Into the world for those still here, and in serving feel delight!

The time is *now* to reflect soberly on life, with needed persistence,
To quieten the mind and to contemplate basic realities of existence:
Precious opportunities; impermanence; intention, action, and result;
And the weaknesses of earthly life, are four crucial thoughts to exalt!

These will shift our interest from short-term worldly concerns,
Toward everlasting insights, for which the heart truly yearns.
We may come to conclude that a spiritual path is needed,
Since results of our present deeds in the next life must be heeded.

The fact that we all from family and friends will one day part,
And leave everything we possess here, we must take to heart.
The soul will go on and leave its earthly home, the body, behind:
This is the reality, to which we cannot afford to be blind.

Since the law of intention, action and result governs our existence,
To our deeds today, and their effects, we cannot show indifference.
We cannot taste the fruit of good actions that we have not done,
Nor escape consequences of unwise deeds done under the sun.

After death, we'll follow the course traced by our actions, good and bad;
So we mustn't act against our deepest heart desires and then be sad.
As where the body goes, the shadow comes along with it;
Wherever our soul goes, karma follows, that we have to admit.

Now is the time to pray for love, while we are healthy and well,
So we can focus our efforts and not in strife and contention dwell.
But, if we put off prayer until we're sick, suffering, and dying,
Then it'll be much harder, and we may even give up trying!

So, what is needed as the earthly life year by year ebbs away,
Is to seek divine help, keep a good heart, and act loving from day to day,
To be kind to everyone, and be an inspiration,
And to offer heavenward wholesome prayers of aspiration.

Now is the time to positively change the course of things,
When we have the opportunities our life presently brings!
Only in this way we'll be transformed from within and not miss
Reaching a realm of wonderful eternal happiness and bliss

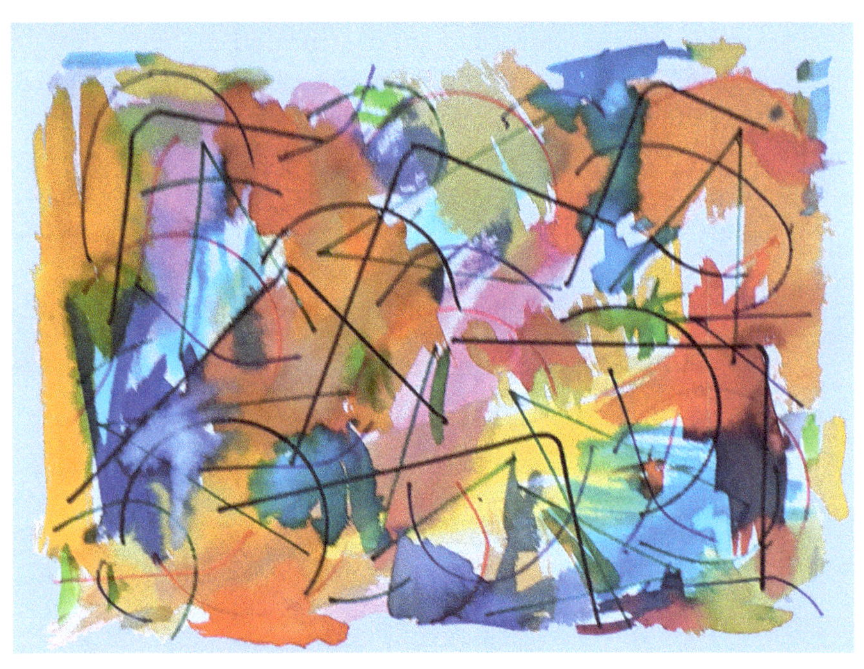

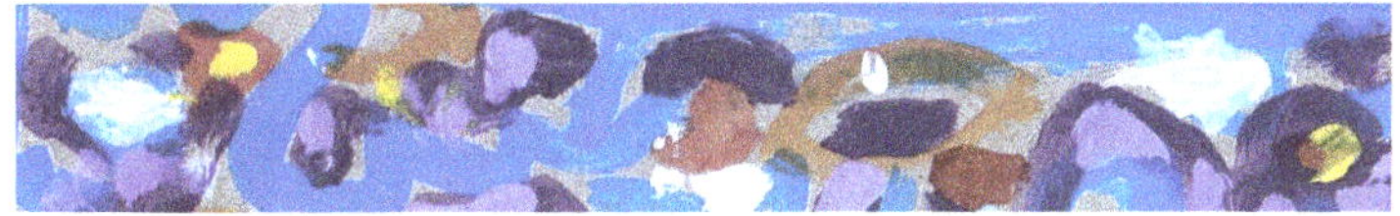

In Memoriam

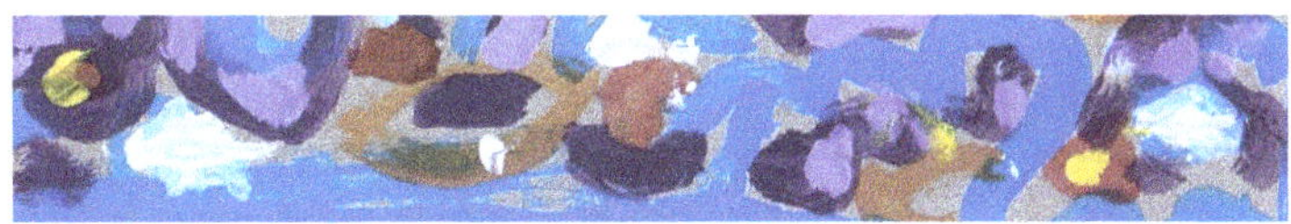

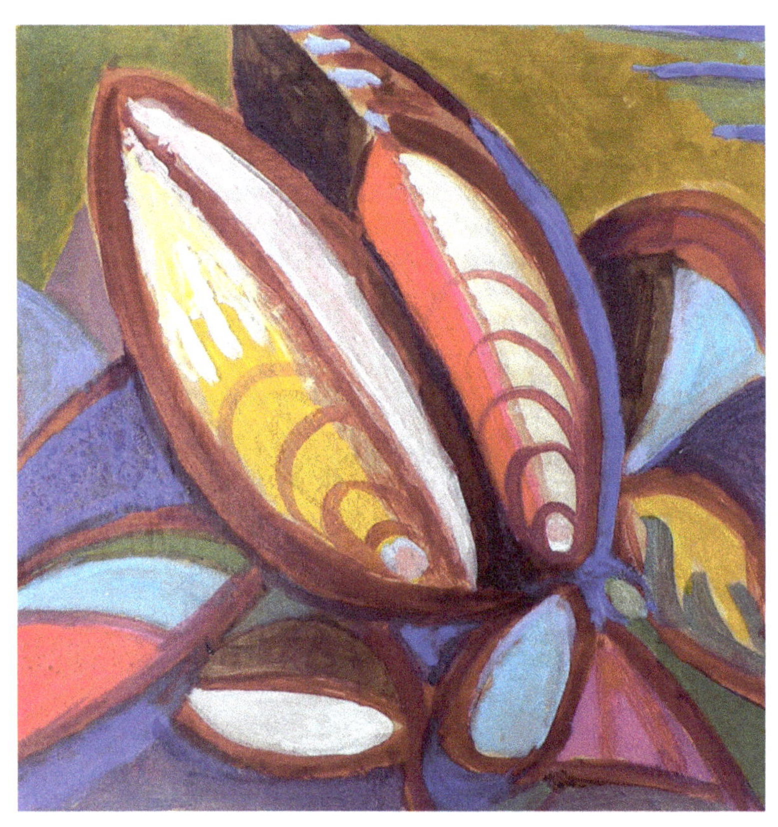

Lynn

Sadly, Lynn passed away a couple of days ago.
That she'd been ill for some time, we did know.
My thoughts went back to a few decades before,
To my mind's eye, memories returned once more.

We were students at a small college,
Dedicated to sound values and knowledge.
How true the words of the well-known song,
To which in listening I have sung along:

"Those were the days my friend,
We thought they'd never end."
Now, reflecting in the quietness of the morning:
Lynn's end came, and for her a new existence is dawning.

How true that all come naked from their mother's womb,
And, as they came, so they depart for their tomb.
How short and fleeting this life is, full of human flaws,
This should make us pause, before our end close draws.

An ancient scribe once wisely wrote,
The essence of which I will now quote:
It is better to go to a place of mourning,
Than to where there's fun and stage performing

For when all in this life is said and done,
Death is indeed the destiny for everyone.
Thinking of Lynn, am I taking this to heart?
Am I ready for when from all I know, I'll be torn apart?

My father-in-law, mid-ninety, often tells us, "Seize the day",
Am I using my time well before I, too, will one day fly away?
May I swiftly come to grips with my own life's meaning,
And quickly from all trivia and folly myself be weaning!

.

May we each soberly reflect on our life's end,
And every day our time in the best manner spend.
Thank you, Lynn, for the life you led and your light;
Your good works, in our memories, keep shining bright.

After this short earthly stay and death, there's a destiny beyond;
But no need here to speculate and to many questions now respond.
May we speedily come to grips with our fragile mortality,
And be ready in peace to confidently face our future reality.

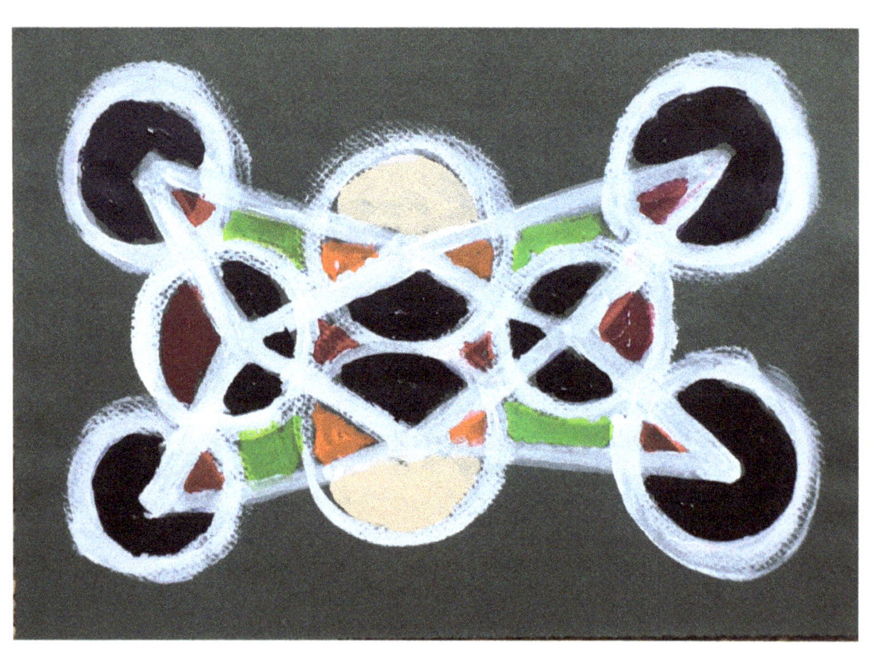

Henry

Remembering Henry Maire,
He was a man with certain flair.
At the golf club we would meet,
From the door he'd wave and greet.

Henry ate at his favourite table,
Then came to us when he was able,
With a cup of coffee in his hand;
Our chats were never bland.

Henry was a well-versed man,
Who travelled to many a land,
A trying health issue him didn't defeat,
He always came across upbeat.

He wrote his memoirs in a book.
His vignettes warrant a closer look.
Partly his joys and sorrows we all share;
He was a man who for others did care.

We remember his last Club good-bye,
He had a concern for a friend nearby.
Henry's kind smile and good cheer
Warmed hearts of those far and near.

In many ways, he was very gifted,
Always leaving us uplifted.
Henry's earth life has reached its ending,
But, his consciousness is unending!

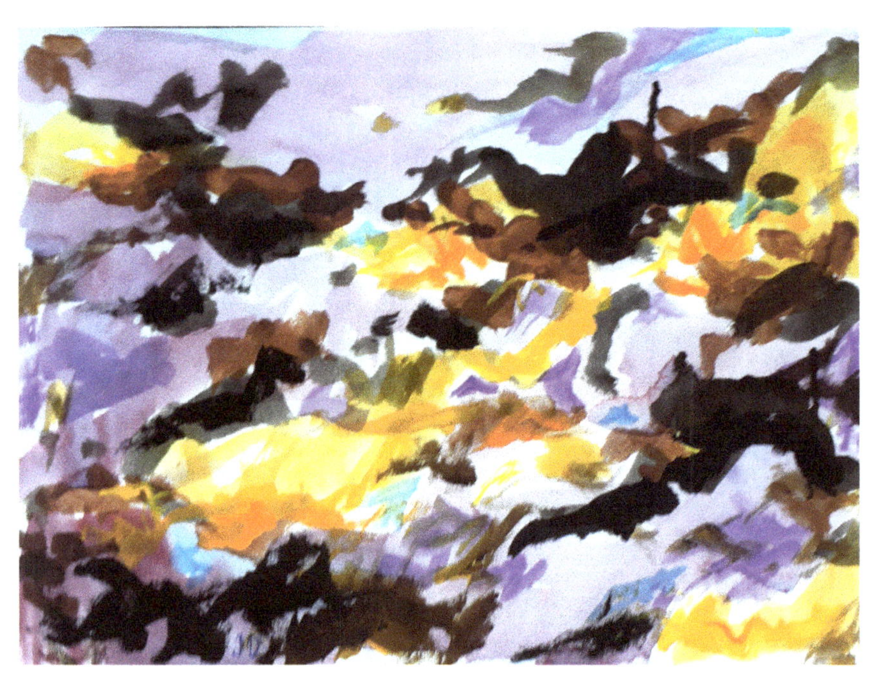

Maria

Upon our many a Hütteldorferstrasse stay,
Helga so kind was, we must say.
We saw love, warmth in her eyes,
That goes beyond human ties.

One summer day, outside we all enjoyed her food,
Among us all, there was a wonderful mood.
In that fleeting flash of time,
Her joy and sparkle were sublime.

Her earthly body was a just brief abode,
Her mind and soul like a guest on life's road.
Through them Helga is going on,
May she reach a never-ending dawn.

There is much suffering in this life,
As well as a lot of strife.
But in the end, all evil we can turn around,
This, I know, very difficult does sound.

We now have to continue on life's way,
But, none of us here forever will stay.
May we do the very best we can,
Then go on into a life of endless span.

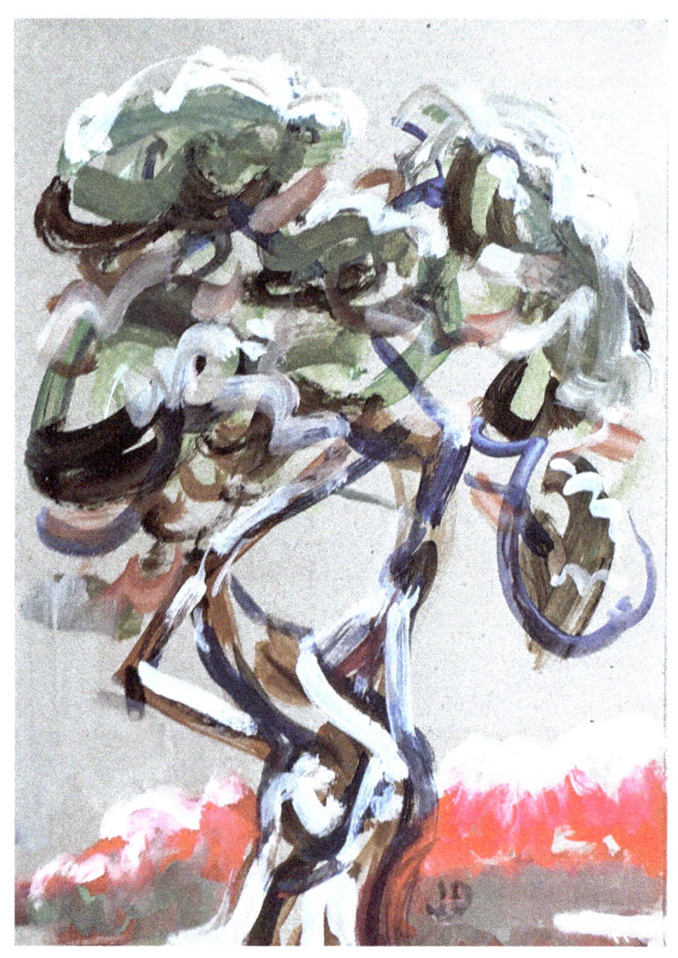

Mourning a Poinciana Tree

With the poinciana tree in view, I'd at my window sit,
Starting the day in meditation made the tree a perfect fit.

Yesterday morning, the tree loppers came,
Watching them made me feel almost lame.
In one roaring chainsaw cut, the green tree fell!
Now I grieve as if under some kind of a spell.

On many hot summer days in years gone by,
Bright red flowers stood out against the blue sky.
Now just an empty space – it makes me sigh,
I take a deep breath, but could almost cry.

In a way, life is like the now gone poinciana tree.
We come to earth – to make choices we are free.
Hopefully we grow, bloom, and to others bring cheer,
Till the day we leave behind those who to us are dear.

With a good heart and actions sweet,
May we our purpose of serving others meet,
And the most of this brief earthly existence make,
For one day, our last breath we all will take.

We are on this planet for just a short time;
To waste it would be sad and almost a crime!
But, if we have used our opportunities well,
There is no way of the future glory to tell!

Like the tree, we too may meet an unexpected end.
So let's not take things for granted as we often tend!

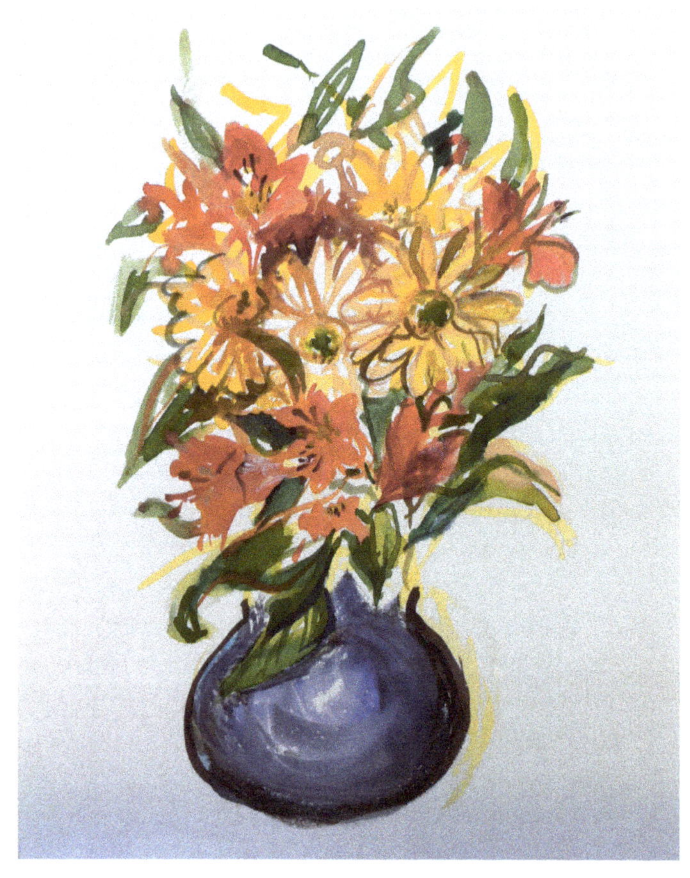

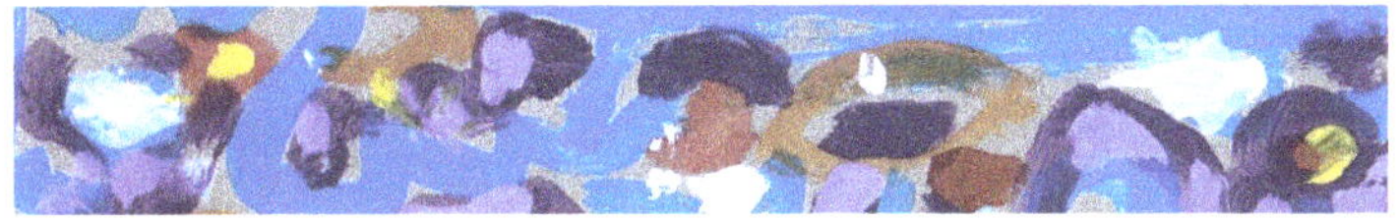

Friendship

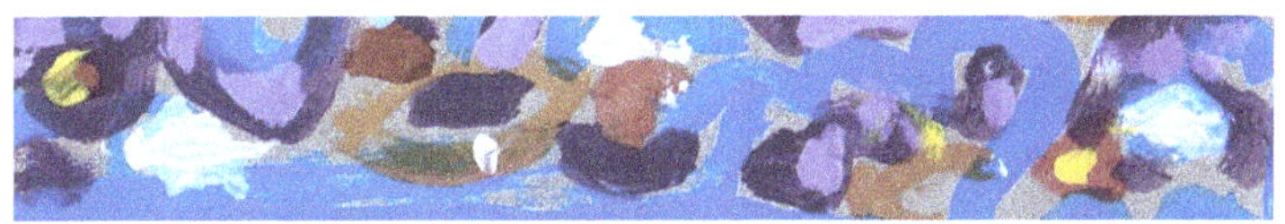

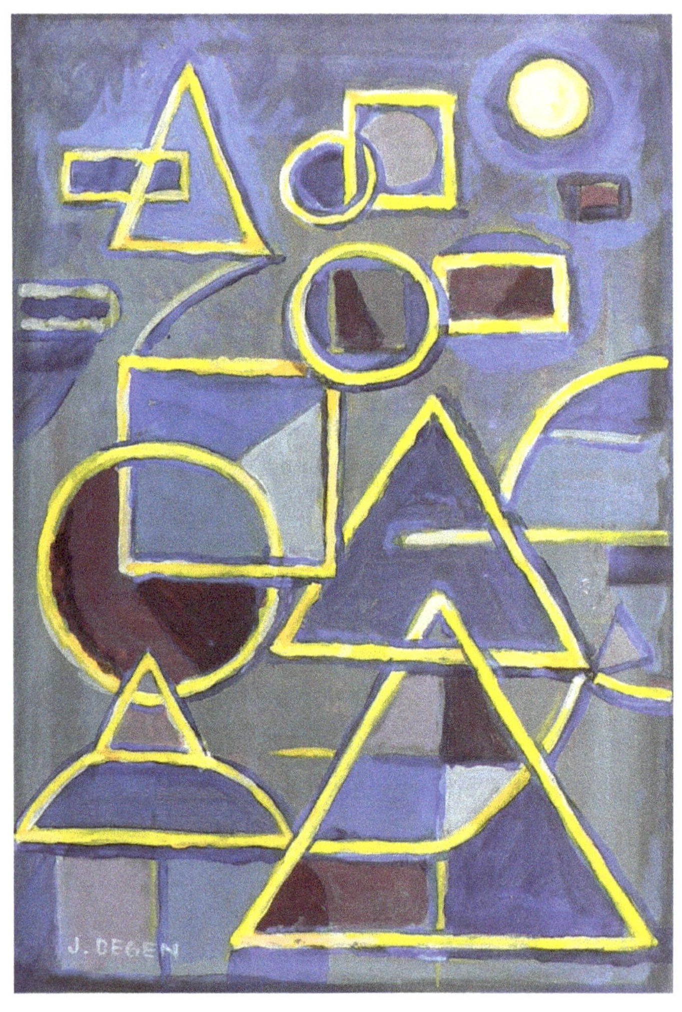
J. DEGEN

To an Aged Friend

Our dear friend, we remember you today;
May your faith stay strong, come what may!

Your days may now feel dull and long;
In your mind, may you remain strong.

In your long life, you've been very kind;
May you leave any regrets truly behind.

Be forgiving toward one and all,
And peace upon you surely will fall.

All your worries take into prayer,
Then in faith, rest with little care.

May you have joy, peace, and love,
As you await what is above!

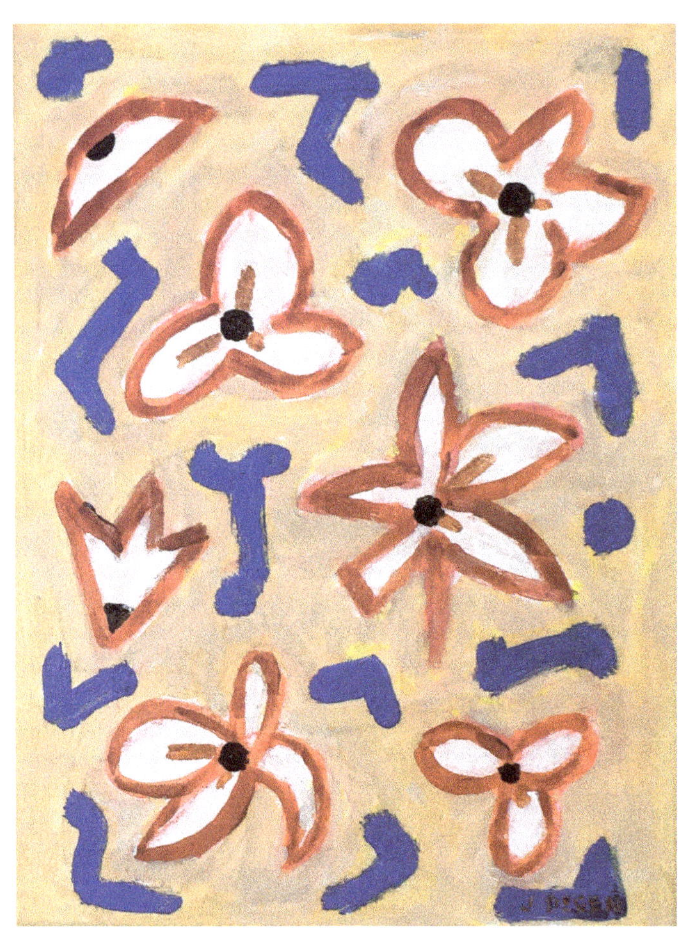

To Friends of Long Ago

Calling you after many years at the same home was a thrill,
Hearing you both speak, it was as if time had stood still!

After a long time, to know that you're both keeping well,
Was a delight to hear; may you continue thus to dwell!

A lovely couple you are, we have often said.
And indeed, an interesting life you have led.

You are a special husband and wife,
Who now have had a fairly long life.

May you both have many more fulfilling years,
And not be troubled by unfounded, nagging fears.

May you be filled with faith and devotion,
Which saints of old had deep as the ocean.

May your love for each other continue to grow;
From which many good fruits will further flow.

We would like to wish you both the very best;
May your lives together with harmony be blessed!

We'll leave you the following blessing and prayer today;
May the words be fulfilled in your lives in a special way!

In all your days, may you both be happy and well,
And free from sadness which can hang over us like a spell.

Indeed, may you experience an inner bliss that knows no sorrow;
And have peace within, no matter what comes tomorrow!

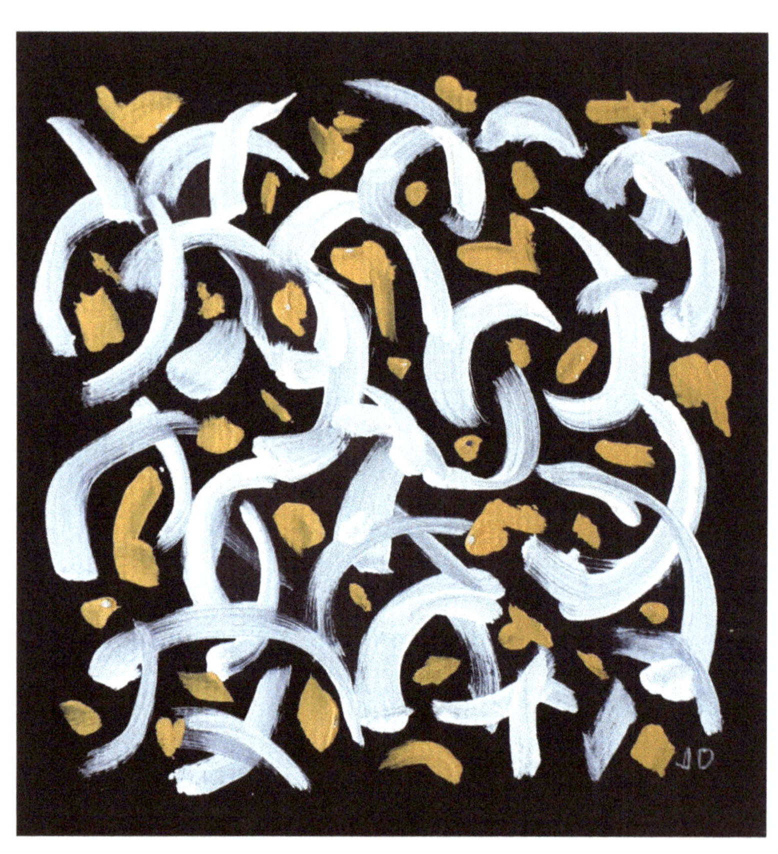

144

To a Friend in Sickness

Sorry to hear you are not well;
What life will bring, one cannot tell.

We hope that you'll soon be on the mend,
May your illness swiftly come to an end.

Thank you for your past work for us all;
We know your effort and sacrifice weren't small.

In your last talk you told us to stay positive;
Indeed, this is great advice on how to better live.

Of course, we hope to see you again before long,
Perhaps even whistling or humming a happy song!

Good bye for now, and please take care;
May someone soon good news about you share!

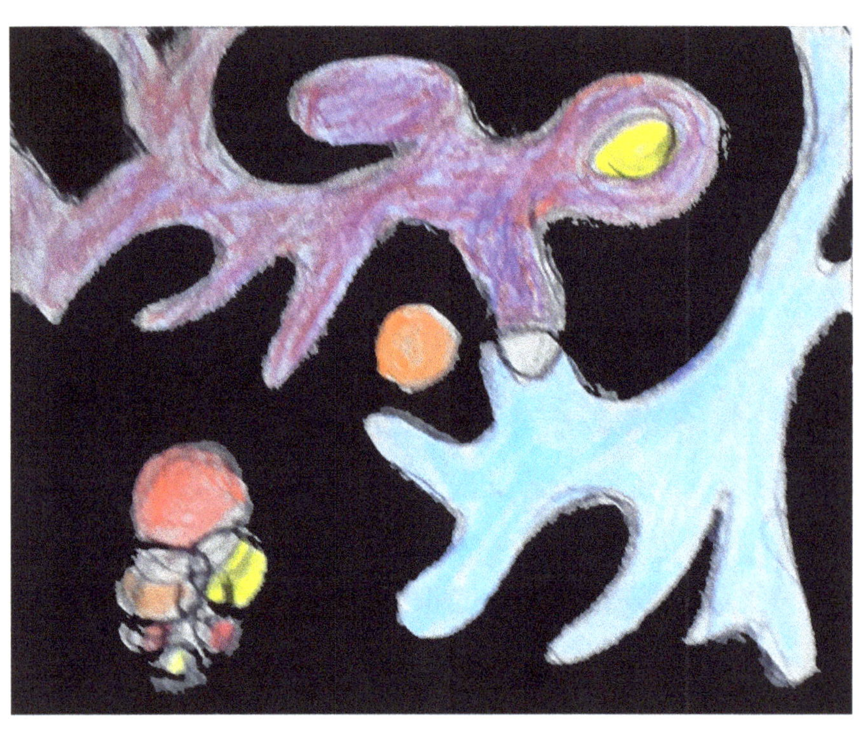

Keeping in Touch

We hope that you are keeping well,
What life may bring, we cannot tell.

Life does have its ups and downs,
Our deeds sometimes cause frowns.

This little note is to stay in touch;
Things to do there is always much!

We'll end with these thoughts of you;
And go back to things we must do.

We hope that you have a successful day,
Gracefully dealing with come what may.

We wish you all the very best;
May your life be truly blessed.

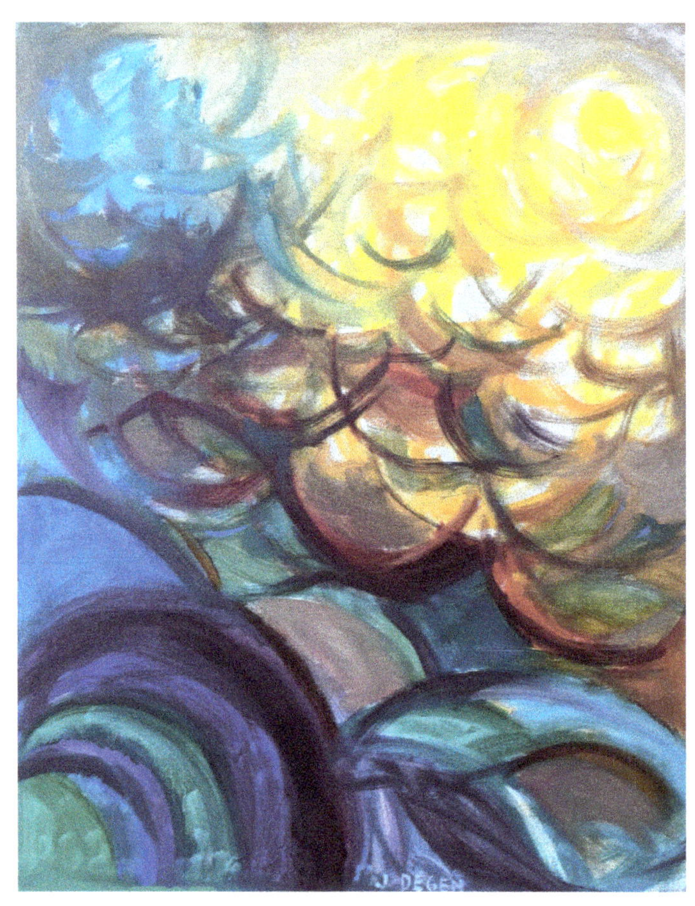

Happy Birthday in Hospital

Come what may on your special day,
As you can, enjoy your birthday!
In life, we can't always have our way,
And that's sometimes to our dismay.

On your birthday, may you have some cheer,
Maybe they'll let you have a sip of beer.
On all your days, steer clear of any fear,
No matter what from anyone you may hear.

We never know what'll happen in our life,
Good or bad times, ill health or strife.
But, you've a loving wife by your side,
Who has with you laughed and cried.

Despite all, we wish you all the best,
Sincerely, and certainly not in jest.
Take care and stay positive, our friend,
And trust that it'll all work out in the end!

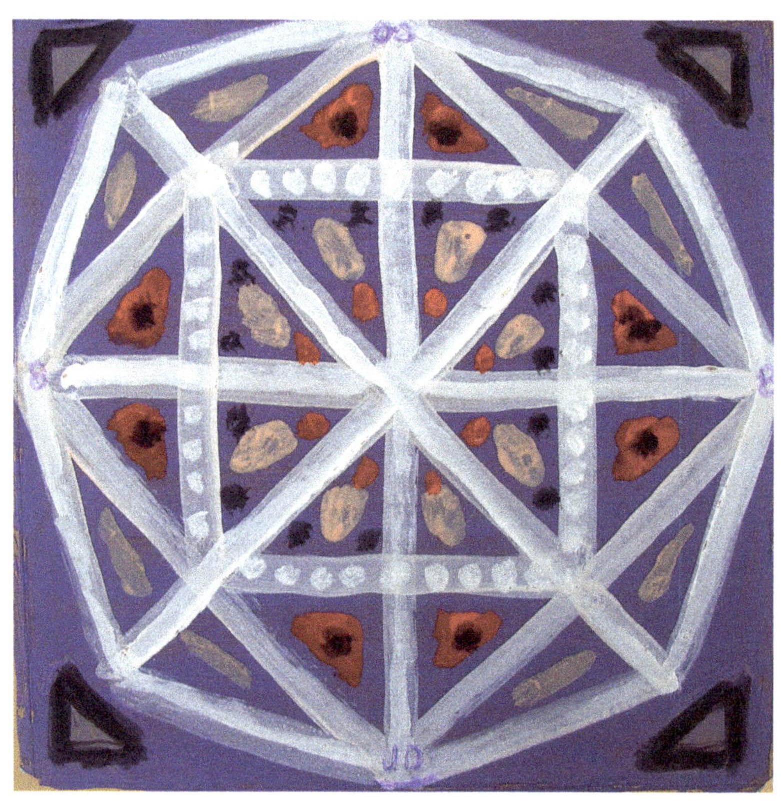

Nonagenarian Birthday

Congratulations are due on your birthday;
May it turn out to be a special day.
We hope that it will a day of cheer,
In looking back on another year.

A singer sang the words, "Oh, my,
Just how quickly the time does fly!"
Last year you were ninety-four;
Of course, with life's end near the door.

This year you've reached ninety-five;
We're all glad you're still alive.
Life's ups and downs you have been through;
Yet, those that reach your age are few!

Some writers mention "threescore and ten",
But you've made it long past then!
Still, one never knows, the poet wrote with insistence,
"Tomorrow here, or in your next existence!"

No-one can tell which it will be,
So readiness is behoved of you and me.
We never know what comes into our days;
May you be protected in all your ways.

"Seize the day!" we've heard wise men say;
Better advice has seldom come our way!
So in the present, give your life the best;
Then in the hereafter you'll surely be blessed!

No matter what this day may bring,
Treat yourself to some special thing.
Despite everything, may this poem give you a lift;
It's from all of us, to you, a little gift!

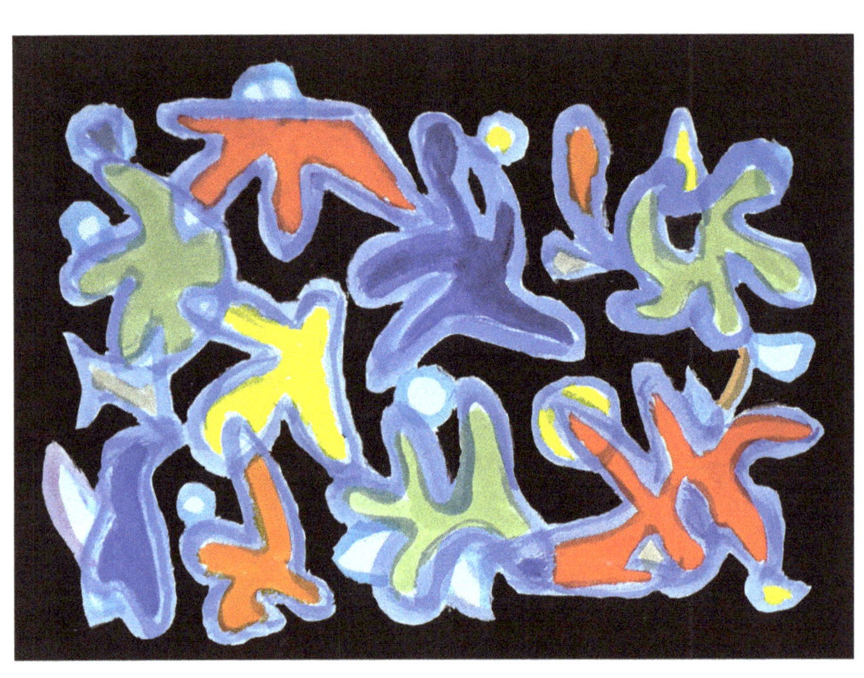

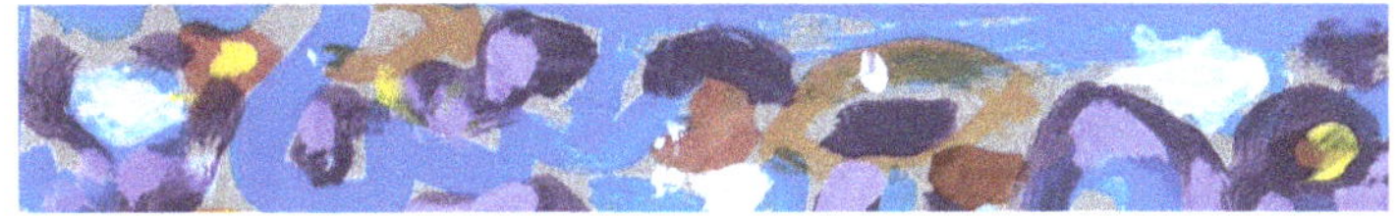

Family

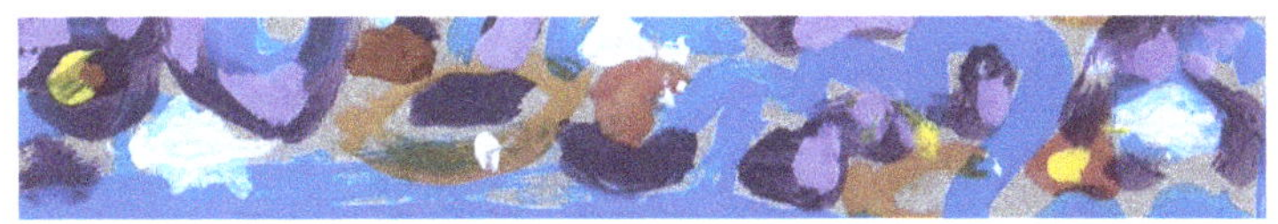

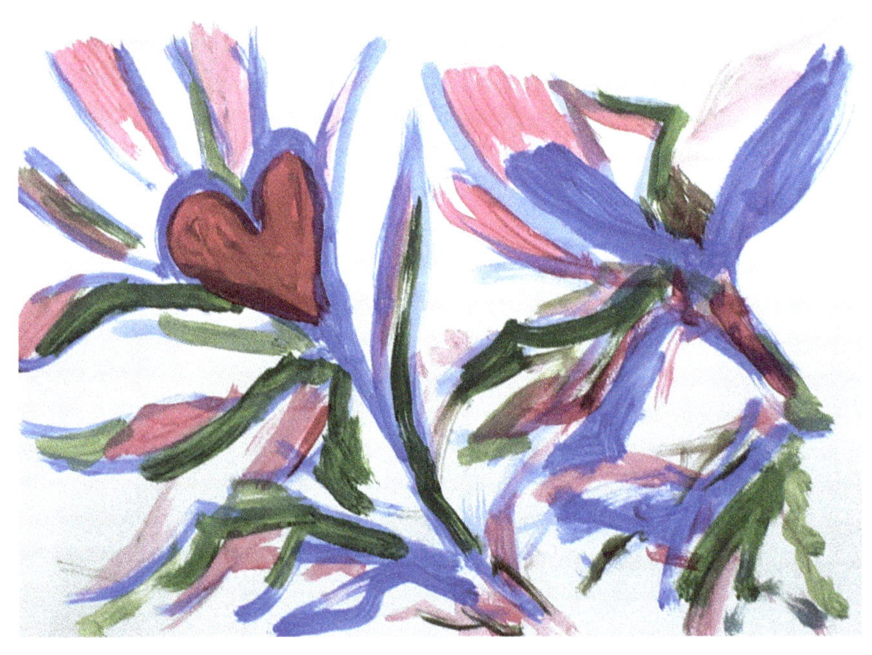

Wife's Birthday

What a wonderful wife you have been,
Precious daily love I've always seen!

You are one in a thousand as the Bible does show,
From you such wonderful qualities do abundantly flow!

You are indeed a special being,
Your faithfulness I keep non-stop seeing!

Your life has been a delightful light,
For this many examples I could cite!

Thank you for the many kind things you do,
And with your word you always come through!

Thank you for your thoughtful goodwill,
And how you tackle each task with skill!

You've been blessed with remarkable health,
Keep doing all you can to protect this wealth!

May you always further abound
In three qualities that are forever sound:

In faith, hope, and most importantly love;
And always be peaceful like a gentle dove!

Whatever trials may come your way,
Just remain strong without undue dismay.

Of the five mind poisons be fully aware,
For then in your life you'll far better fare!

Beware of hatred, greed, jealousy, and pride,
Also keep ignorance far from your side!

May today, your birthday, be a lovely day,
Enjoy it thoroughly in each and every way!

We're also sharing a special lunch with your Dad,
A blessing that can sure make our hearts glad!

Congratulations are due on your 65th birthday,
With thanks for your love – what more can I say?!

These words are written with great gratitude;
They're far from just being a platitude!

So, all the very best for today and always.
May love, joy, and peace fill all your days!

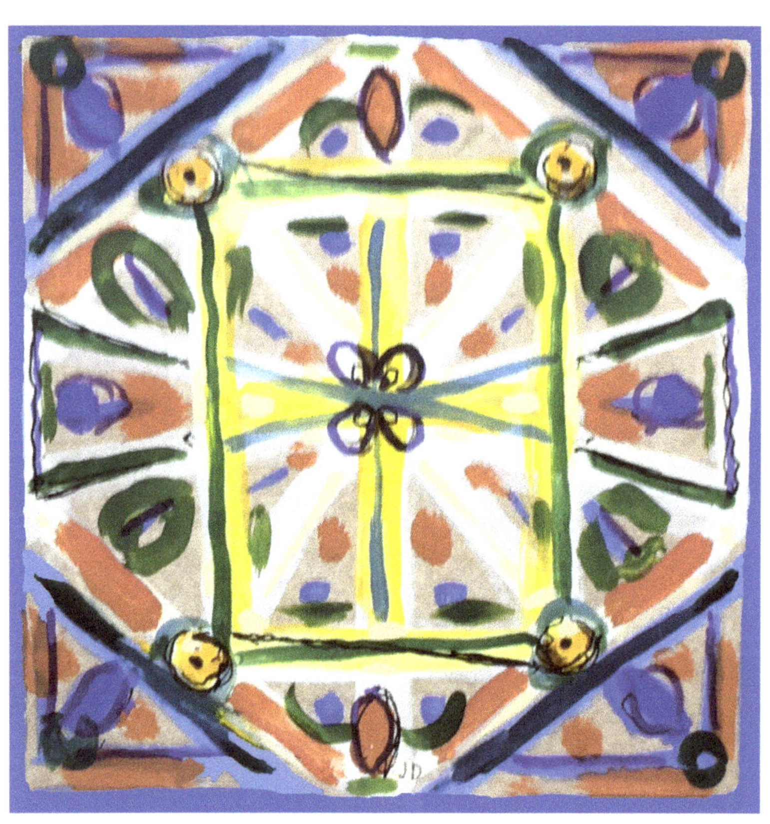

Husband's Birthday

You are turning sixty-eight,
That's a reason to celebrate!
Much to be grateful for in this life,
Most of all, to be your wife!

May your life continue to be great,
And may you long remain my mate!
Even though the years go fast,
Let's not focus on the past!

Each moment we can together create,
Full of love and never hate.
Start our days with a loving touch,
And filled with gratitude for much.

Let this be a special day,
Packed with bliss along the way.
Even though life is uncertain,
On joy we don't have to draw the curtain.

Enjoy the here and now to the full,
In the right way – don't be a fool!
There is much beauty all around,
Focus on what won't drag you down.

Though you aren't far from the "threescore and ten",
And much can happen before then,
A grand future life you can for yourself create,
If you on the spiritual concentrate.

"Seize the day!" we've heard my father say;
Very wise advice that's come our way!
So, in the present, give your life the best;
Then in the hereafter you'll surely be blessed!

May you have a wonderful year!
Take what comes with no undue fear.
As you virtues pursue and on what's good meditate,
May your life's path as much as possible be kept straight.

May you receive wisdom when challenges arise,
And may they us not overwhelm or demoralize.
May love and joy transcend any sorrow,
For we have much to look forward tomorrow!

Let's celebrate this birthday with my mate,
Doing something special on a date!

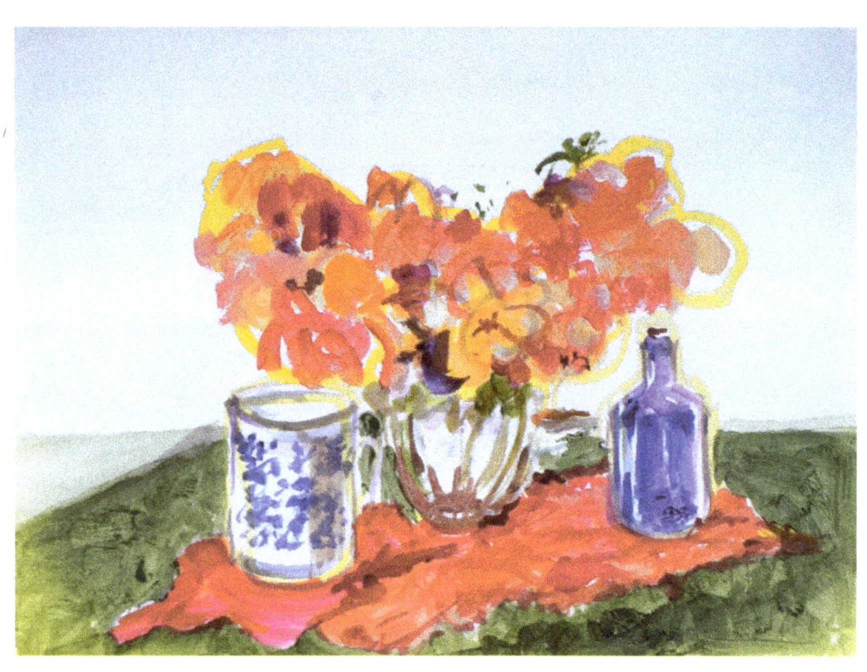

Anniversary Poem

What a wonderful wife you are,
From being perfect, you're not far!

But, of course, there's still work to do,
And that's true for everyone else too.

Such a superb example you set,
Very few people like you I have met.

Attractive in body, mind, and spirit;
Your character qualities royalty befit!

I hope these lines don't cause pride to rise;
That could surely begin your demise!

But of this, may I have little fear;
Let your love continue to shine clear.

Then humility there will be,
Such as is fitting of nobility.

Our days and nights are flying by;
My, oh my, how the time does fly!

Thank you so much for all you do;
How I truly appreciate you!

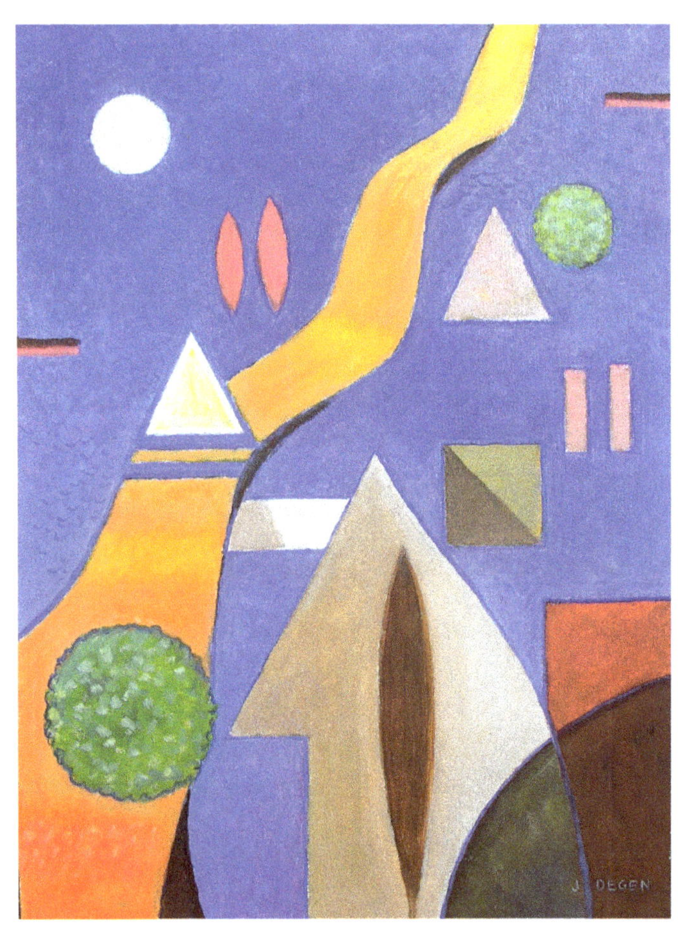

Aged Father's Birthday

Let it be a special day,
Filled with joy along the way.

Amazing! You're now ninety-four!
The end of life stands at the door.

Thanks for all the love you've shown,
To us and others you have known.

Thank you for your joy and cheer,
May it continue all year.

Though some hardships you have had,
You've remained a positive dad!

We never know what comes into our days;
May you be protected in all your ways.

May you go on having joy,
As life's beauties you enjoy.

May each day add to a wonderful year!
Take what comes with no undue fear.

We wish you happiness on your special day,
With much love and peace along the way!

An Afterthought

Some say that there is no future day;
But, evidence points the other way.

Sooner or later, we'll each leave our earthly dwelling;
For our future, a universal rule is compelling:

We will all reap what in this life we have sown;
Even now on the earth, this truth can be shown.

May we wisely sow good words and deeds in this life,
To have fortunate circumstances in the afterlife!

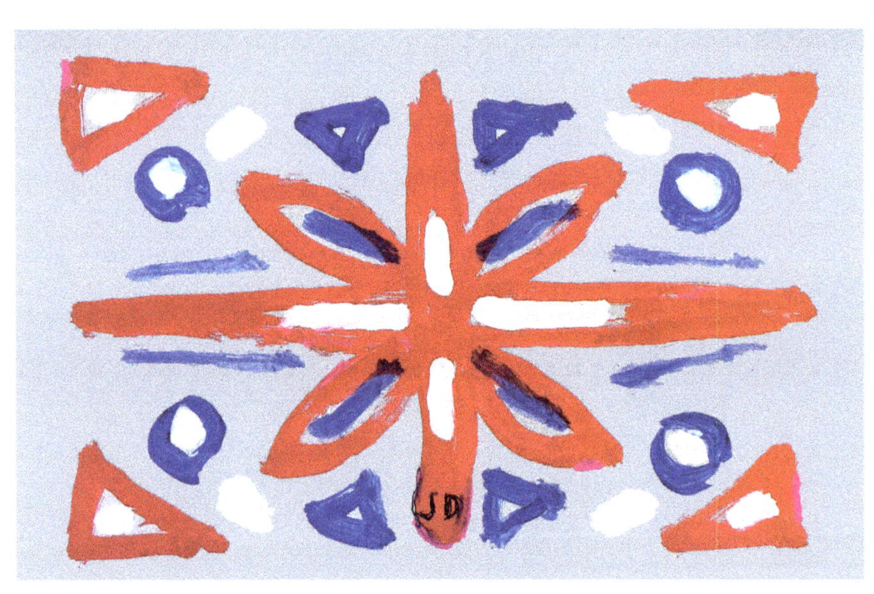

New Year's Wish for Dad

We wish you a happy New Year,
Even in hard days, to find some cheer.
Luckily you have good friends near,
So hopefully there'll be less to fear.

Another year! How the time does fly!
Soon we'll all leave and say good-bye.
No-one is here forever to stay,
We all know well it is that way.

This coming year, stay in good health,
May nothing destroy or steal this wealth.
May you have a deep peace of mind,
Unlike those who this yet need to find.

May your art and creativity soar,
With never a moment that is a bore!
May your days be lived in good mood,
With little time given to brood.

If hardships arrive for a season,
Know that there must be a reason.
Stay positive in the days ahead,
May there be nothing to ever dread.

You have set us a good example,
To emulate you, there is ample.
A good man like you isn't easy to find,
You are one of a special kind.

May this be a very good year,
One that you'll always hold dear.

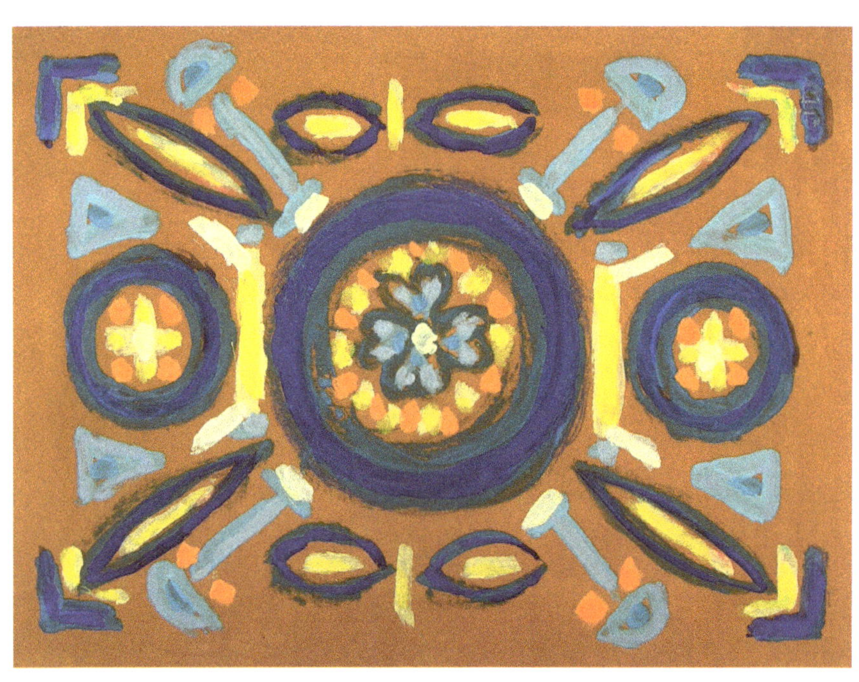

Heartfelt New Year's Wish

Another new year is soon going to dawn;
And, we never know what it may spawn.

Our personal future of course we can't foretell.
Yet, whatever happens, we truly wish you well.

May you yet enjoy reasonably good health.
This, without a doubt, is a wonderful wealth!

May you see all your needs graciously met;
And may no relationships bother you or cause upset.

May you have peace of mind and lasting contentment,
And never harbour the poison of any resentment.

May your home remain a quiet and secure place,
Where you always like returning to as your base.

So, as we wish you the customary "happy New Year",
May you experience well-being, without needless fear.

May patience, forgiveness, and tolerance each be your guide;
And may also faith, hope, and love with you abide.

As we end our lines, we wish you all the very best;
May your life in many ways continue to be blessed.

And, should the hour of departure come to be met,
Stay hope-filled for this fresh beginning you will get!

May death be the doorway for new opportunities to expect,
Based on your good fruits from the law of cause and effect.

Keep taking good care of yourself always;
And, may you yet have many happy days!

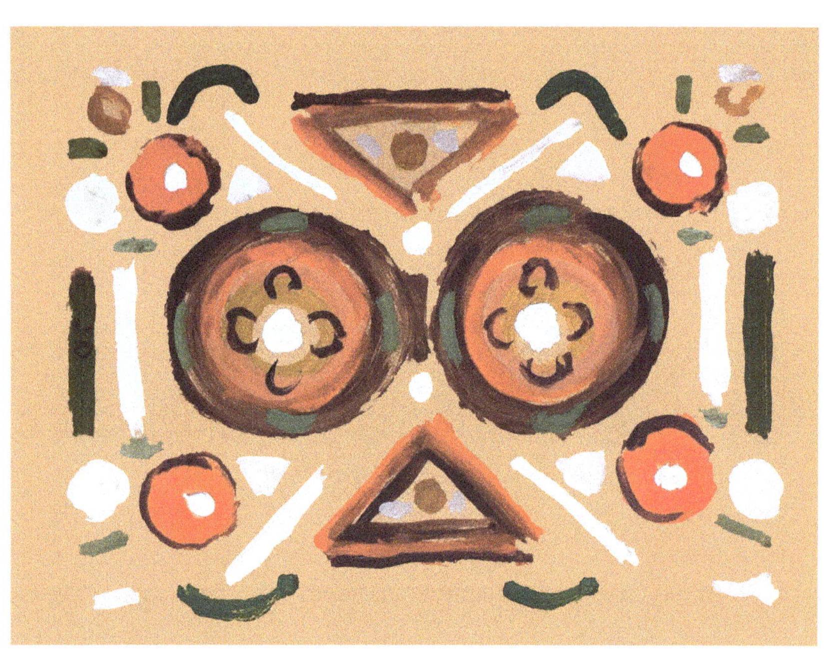

Father's Day

We have another nice opportunity,
As we again meet together in unity,
To thank you on this annual Father's Day,
For your love and care in many a good way!

We thank you for all your kindness,
Which to our lives brings sweetness!
We're grateful for the lunches you've treated us to,
And the special places to enjoy a dessert with you!

You have enriched our lives in numerous ways,
May you keep well and happy in all your days.
We're glad you're still in such good health,
That, by itself, is truly great wealth!

For this Father's Day, we wish you the best,
May what you do and create truly be blessed.

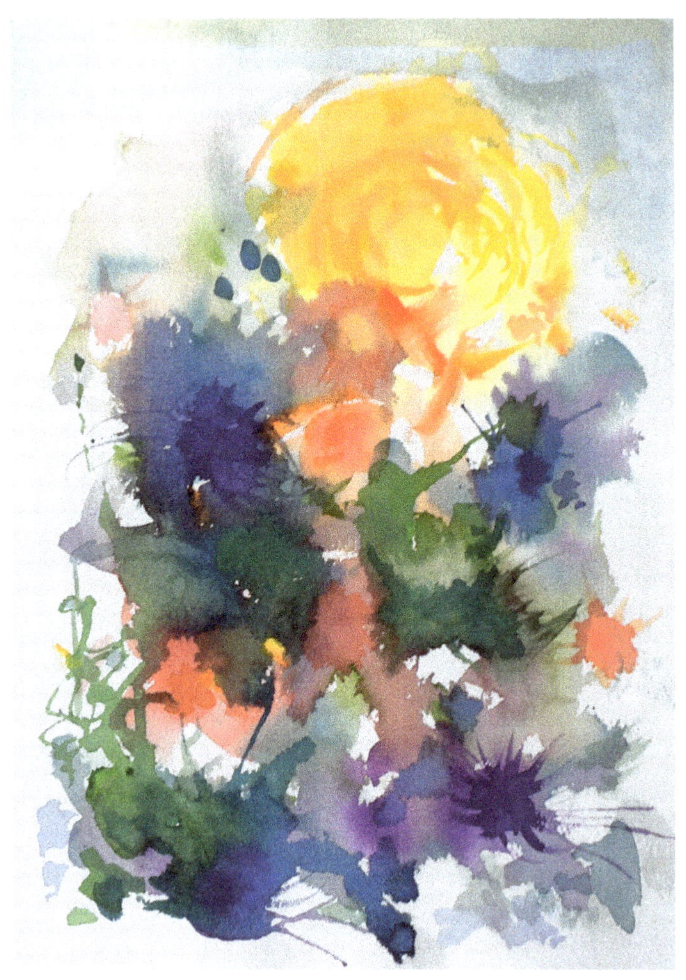

Father's Day Outing

While we together have this beautiful day,
This is what to you we wanted to say:
We truly appreciate your gentle presence,
As well as your heart's loving essence.

To ponder a bit about life on a day like this,
Can cause us the mystery of our being not miss!
We're all here on this earth for a longer or shorter stay,
Then the time comes to continue on our beyond-here way.

Even though our journey through death isn't clear,
There's one thing that we can all truly hold dear:
Looking at life closely, we can see it with love infused,
Despite the pain and suffering that often leave us confused.

Therefore, we can embrace our future with hope,
Which will greatly help us with any fears to cope!
This powerful reality of love and compassion,
Will, in the end, subdue man's misguided passion.

So, on this day, we recall your "Carpe Diem" advice,
Words that at any time and setting can make us wise!
You set us a precious example in your life,
One filled with peace and a lack of strife!

In the ups and downs of life, you tend to remain calm,
For those around you, that's like a healing balm.
To many others, you always express goodwill,
Helping where you can, not wishing anyone ill.

It is inspiring how your life's race you have run.
May we have a great day today in the winter sun!

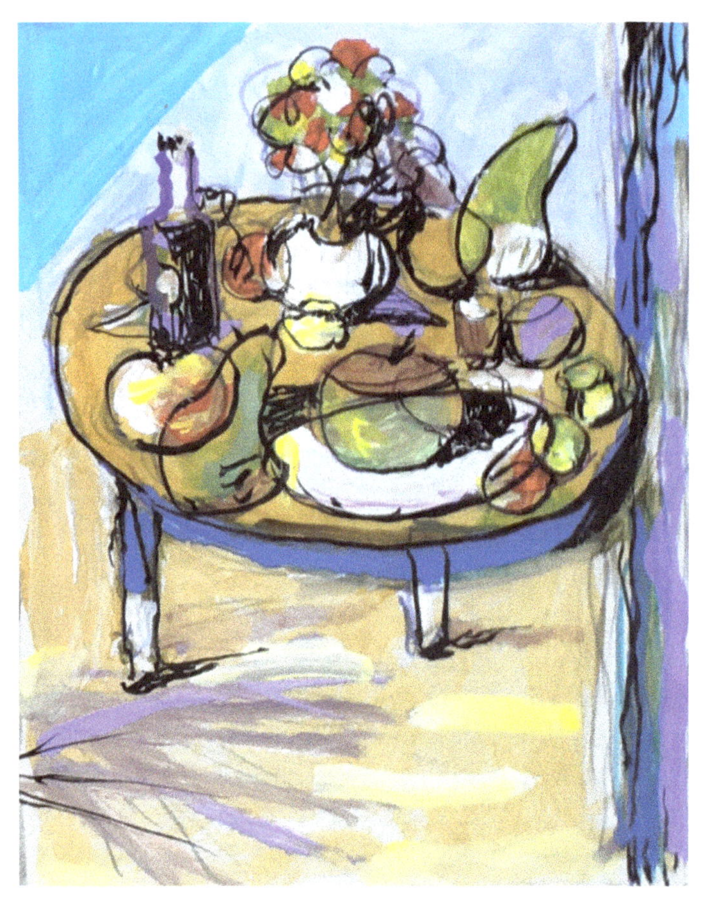

Meals Out with Dad

Once a week, together with dad, we enjoy a meal;
Precious time other tasks can't be allowed to steal.

At times, as we savour the good food,
Peaceful silence may for a while rule the mood.

Just spending time in harmony and peace,
Is a chance in itself each other to please.

Then, as the meal time continues on,
A friendly topic we may touch upon.

Often over coffee and a special cake,
A deeper conversation we begin to make.

Such occasions of heartfelt sharing,
Prompt a feeling of each other's caring.

Over time, strong bonds have been developed;
Vital for times when in problems we are enveloped.

Looking back, indeed life is fleeting,
So "Carpe Diem" is worth repeating.

We all part with friendly smiles;
It was worth travelling the miles.

Then we go our separate ways,
Till our shared meals on future days.

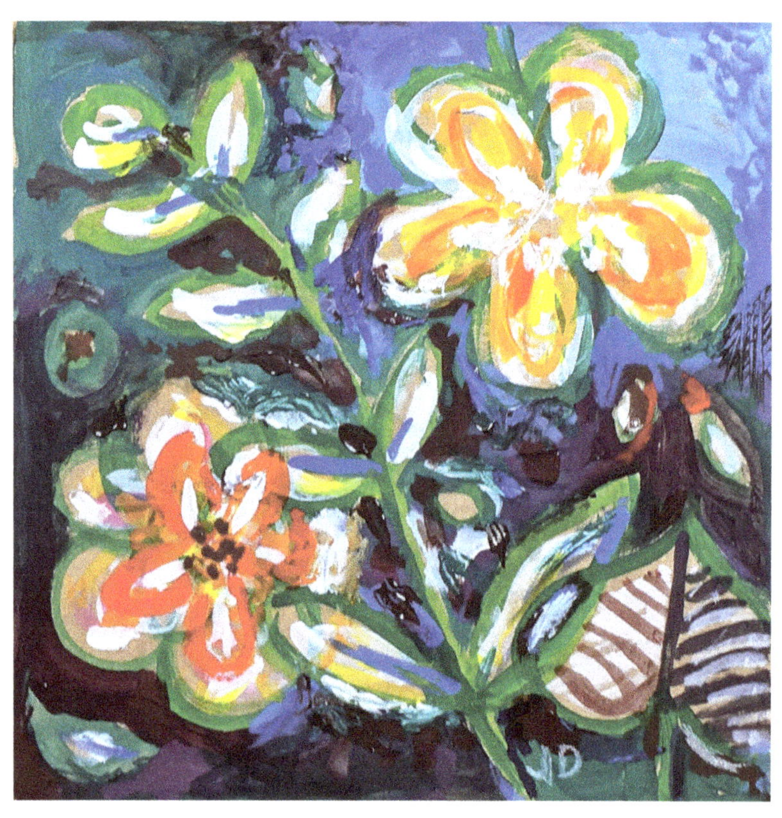

Mother's Day

It is only later in life that I understand,
How much you gave me with a generous hand.

I didn't know you had your own pain and sorrow;
Growing up, I only focused on my tomorrow.

As with all mothers, you had great dreams for me;
May they yet in their own perfect way all come to be!

In my early years, you sacrificed so much;
Sadly, I never fully saw your loving touch.

For many years, you worked all day with many a long hour,
So that upon me whatever I needed you could shower.

Please forgive me for having brought you some sadness;
With my own struggles, I sometimes acted as though with madness.

You never wanted anything but the best for me,
In growing up that I did not always see.

Later in life, thank you so much for visiting us overseas;
Those times live in my mind as very happy memories.

Thank you for helping to create a home secure and stable;
You and my dear dad did for me all that you were able.

May my life in every way bring you honour and joy,
For all the love and compassion you showed your boy!

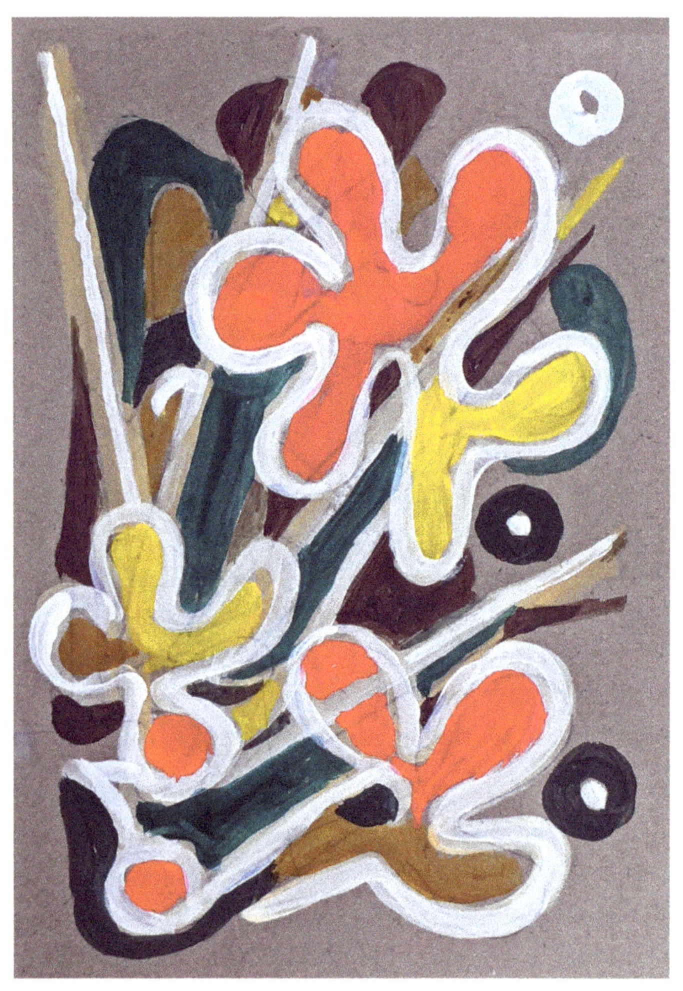

To Mother-in-Law

How short and fleeting is this life of ours,
Soon our body returns to the earth with flowers.

My time spent with you was ever so brief,
That it is now almost beyond belief!

You were the mother of my dear wife;
Thank you for providing for her in early life.

In her frequent sickness, you nursed her to health,
The value of which she daily sees as great wealth.

You took her to ballet lessons for many years,
And guided her practice at home despite her tears.

You saved and worked resourcefully for many a long hour,
So that upon her whatever she needed you could shower.

Still with her is your example of frugality,
Which has brought her peace and blessings constantly.

We all have many hopes and dreams,
But life often turns out different it seems!

I'm deeply grateful for you and your life,
Because the reflections of it I see in my wife.

Thank you for your kindness and goodwill to me,
May you be rewarded in ways you can see.

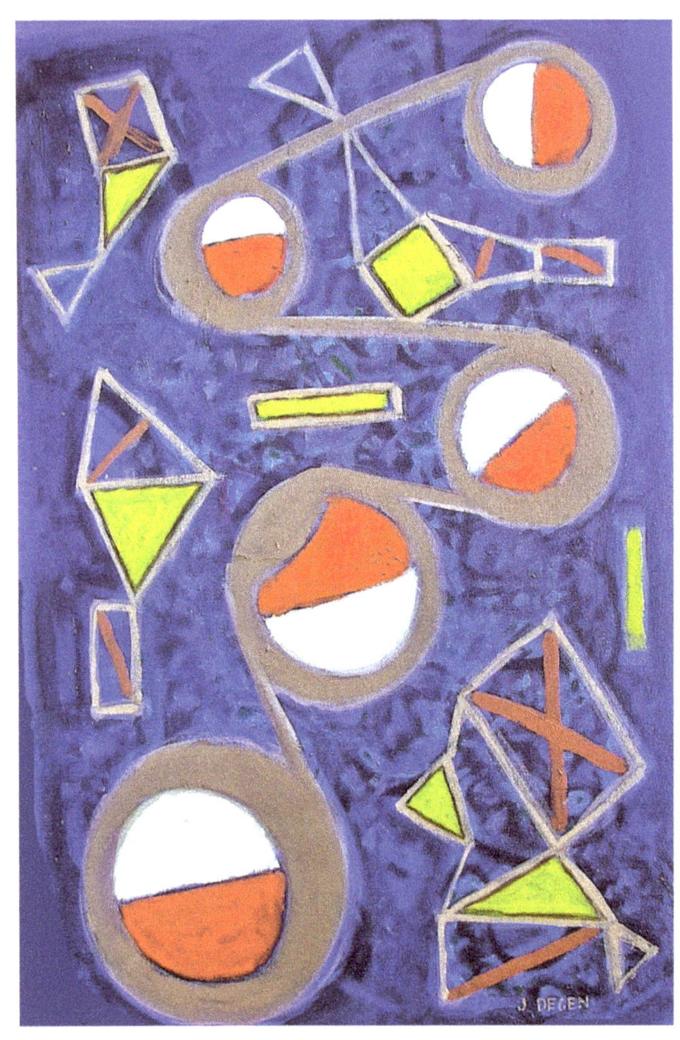

Before a Trip Abroad

May this trip be a special treat,
With lots of precious memories to keep.

May your cross-Pacific flights to and fro
Smoothly, safely and comfortably go!

May you be kept safe all the way,
For this we must diligently pray!

May your fellowship with friends be fine,
With many conversations truly divine!

May your presentation be successful,
And by participants found helpful.

Throughout your trip, may you stay in health;
It is truly a blessing and priceless wealth!

Take some time to think and reflect;
This can even problems help deflect!

Enjoy each day and don't worry about this and that;
I'll be looking after the house, your dad, and cat!

May this trip really enrich your life,
To live in peace, free from all strife!

Make the most of all your time;
This is an opportunity sublime!

Your dad, the cat and I look forward to your return flight,
To again have your wonderful presence in our sight!

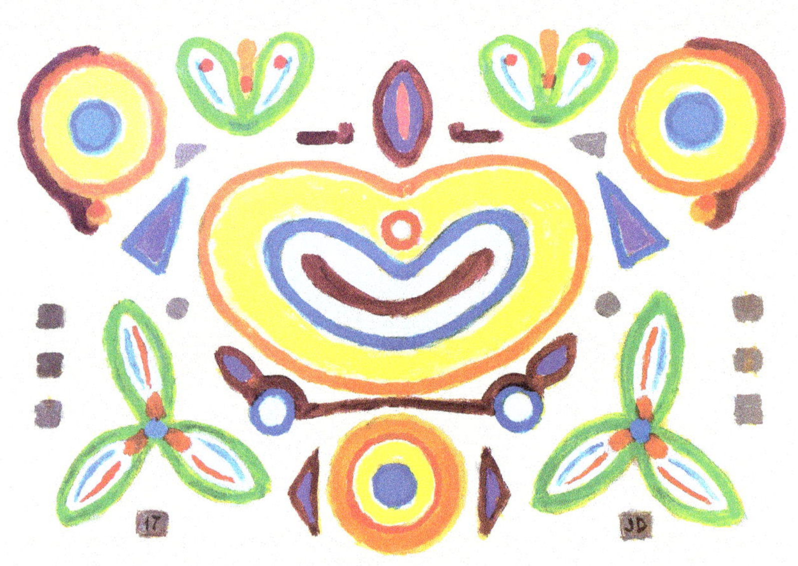

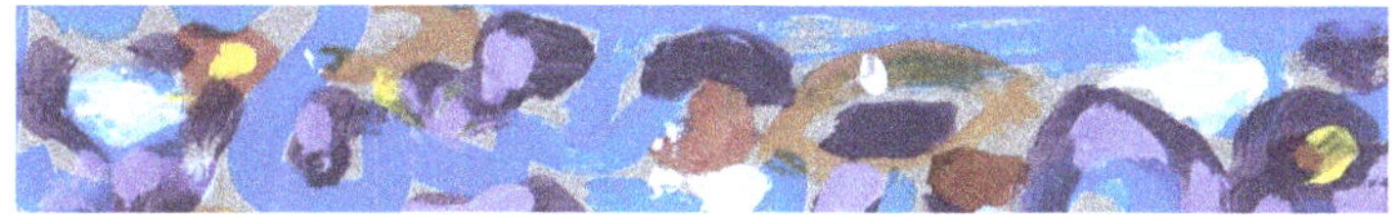

On a Lighter Note

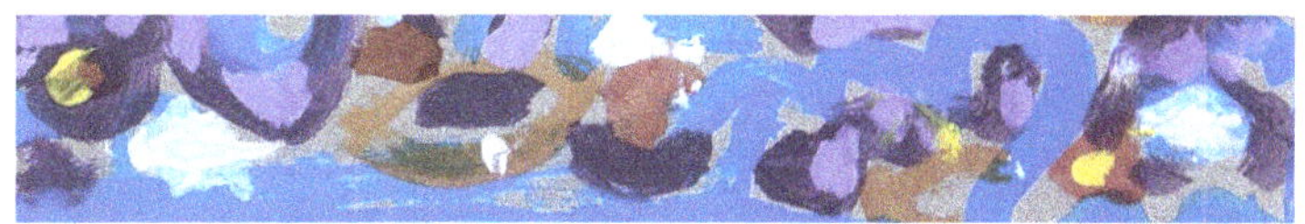

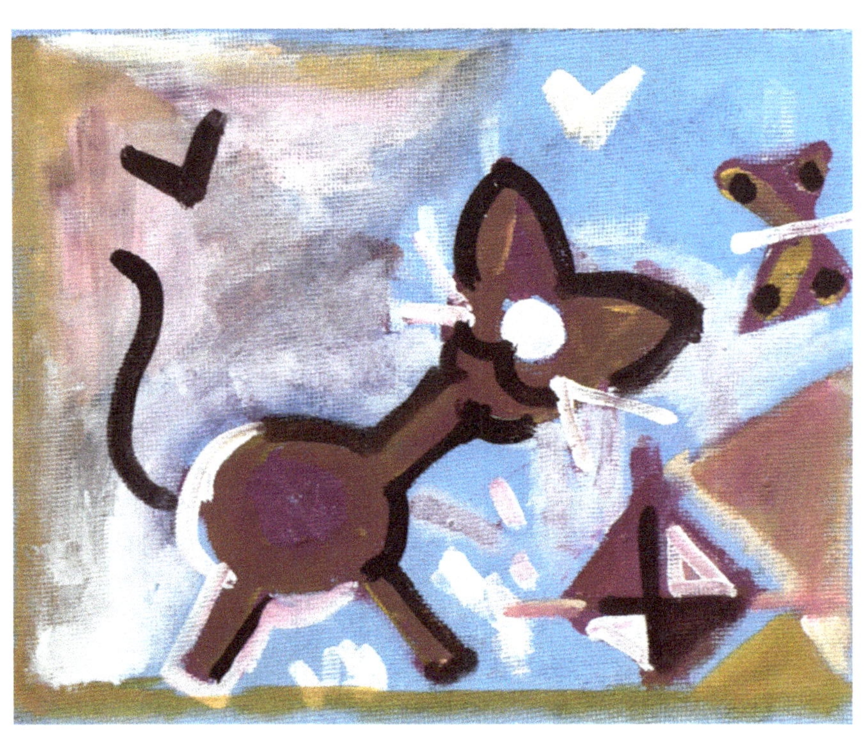

The Neighbours' Cat

Our daily visitor's a special cat,
No-one can really argue about that!
From early morning to late at night,
The cat is always great delight.

She comes early in the morning,
Rattles the door with no warning.
Then gallops in through the door,
Sits and purrs on the kitchen floor.

Before long, she wants a snack,
We some cheese or meat unpack.
At times she gets some chicken meat,
A well-deserved and special treat.

Having relished the tasty food,
She might be in a playful mood.
It's a nice way to start the day,
With some cat fun and watch her play.

Soon thereafter she'll want to sleep,
Her favourite chair we let her keep.
Due to advancing age we say,
She will rest most of the day.

We give bread to birds on the balcony,
This the cat thinks is a felony!
The birds sneak pieces with the cat in sight,
Yell at her, then take to flight.

The cat's been seen enjoying the bread,
Who has ever heard of that?
Then she wants to come inside,
Or under the outside stairs she'll hide.

We bought for her a scratching pole,
So in carpets she makes no hole!
With it she has lots of fun,
Cuddles to it in the sun.

One morning the cat's meow was heard,
In she rushed with a small dead bird!
A bit of shock, this was a topper,
From gift-giving we couldn't stop her!

Somehow, the cat's now our boss,
Without her, we'd be at a loss.
Who'd get us up early each day,
And stop us fall prey to the easy way?

It's years since the cat came our way,
Yet it seems just like yesterday!
She was not always here all day,
This evolved with time some way.

The cat keeps coming to our street side,
That is something we cannot hide.
But our neighbours do not mind,
By nature they are very kind.

It seems this cat has ESP,
How it works is a mystery!
She sensed when we had pain in heart,
brought us comfort, was real smart.

Peacefulness marks her whole life,
There is no unpleasant strife.
Another admirable ability
Is the cat's great equanimity.

The cat is funny just by being,
This we are both daily seeing!
She gives us reason for frequent laughter,
We always feel good thereafter.

She now has less spunk in the morning,
But without her, life'd be boring!
She's an extra special cat,
There is no doubt about that!

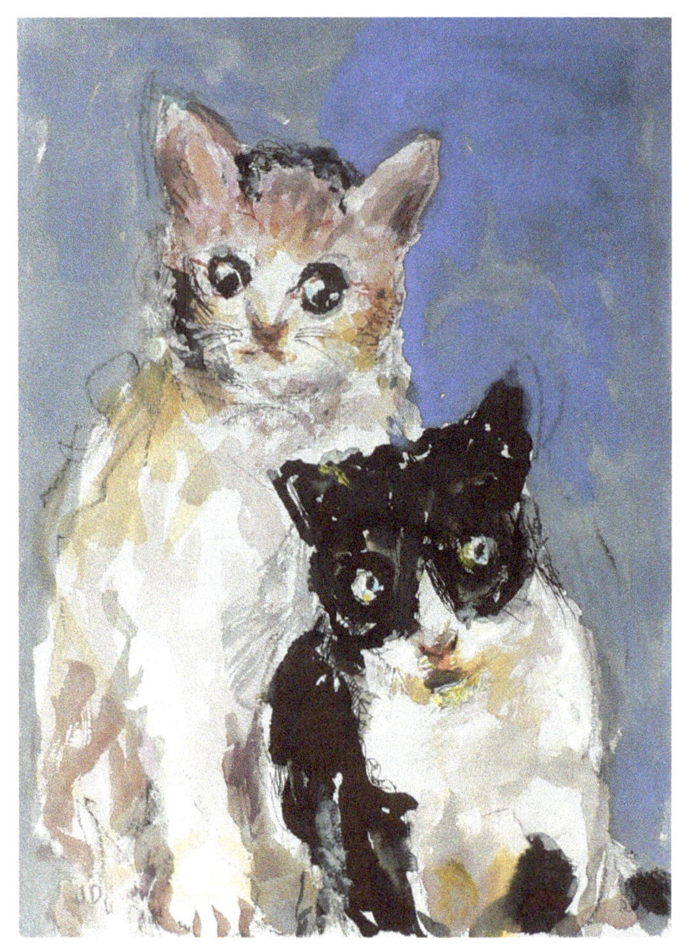

Ode to a Black and White Cat

Our daily visitor's a special cat,
No-one can really argue about that!
Across the road she comes to our side,
From the animals at her house she wants to hide.
Our neighbours do not mind,
By nature they are very kind.
About their cat being with us they are happy,
Their new puppy chased her and was snappy.
So the cat thought, this is no use,
And staying at home she did refuse.

She sensed there was love and kindness here,
Which to her cat heart sounded dear.
She has made herself at home before long,
Bringing us much fun and affection strong.
From early morning to late at night,
The cat is always great delight.
She comes early in the morning,
Rattles the door with no warning.
Then gallops in through the door,
Sits and purrs on the kitchen floor.

Before long, she wants a snack,
We some cheese or meat unpack.
At times she gets some chicken meat,
A well-deserved and special treat.
We give bread to birds on the balcony,
This the cat thinks is a felony!
The birds sneak pieces with the cat in sight,
Yell at her, then take to flight.
The cat's been seen enjoying the bread,
Who has ever heard of that?

A lovable, crazy cat she's indeed.
Sometimes all she wants is eat.
She has a way to beg for a treat,
Our hearts melt and we give her some meat.
Other times the birds' bread makes her happy,
And it then makes her quite peppy.
Her stomach seems like a bottomless pit,
Her diet a noble royal cat would fit.
This truly is a remarkable cat,
Few like her we have ever met.

Having relished the tasty food,
She might be in a playful mood.
It's a nice way to start the day,
With some cat fun and watch her play.
We bought for her a scratching pole,
So in carpets she makes no hole!
With it she has lots of fun,
Cuddles to it in the sun.
Then she wants to go outside,
And under the palms she may hide.

Soon thereafter she'll want to sleep,
Her favourite chair we let her keep.
Due to advancing age we say,
She will rest most of the day.
As she peacefully sleeps on the floor,
I know that one sad day she'll be no more.
In a way, she mirrors human life;
But we won't debate if cats have after-life!
All creatures go from youth, adulthood, to old age and death;
One day, we'll each too on earth take our last breath

It's years since the cat came our way,
Yet it seems just like yesterday!
She was not always here all day,
This evolved with time in some way.
Even though she's now a senior cat,
She still has spunk, we must admit that!
She eats and plays, and goes out and in,
Then she sleeps for hours, stretched out thin.
Or, on the floor curled up next to me,
She is a picture of peace to see.

One morning the cat's meow was heard,
In she rushed with a dead bird!
A bit of shock, this was a topper,
From gift-giving we couldn't stop her!
Another morning we were met
By the cat spraying the hamper wet.
This made us both quite upset,
So out was sent the naughty cat!
But we couldn't long at her be mad,
So back came the cat, no more sad!

On another early morn,
Just around the time of dawn,
The neighbour's other cat came our way,
But was by "our" cat quickly shooed away.
She hissed, growled and made a nasty noise,
It was hard for the tomcat to keep his poise.
So down the stairs he scampered fast,
Then the red mailbox he ran past.
Across the road and up to the roof,
There he then sat and looked aloof.

Somehow, the cat's now our boss,
Without her, we'd be at a loss.
Who'd get us up early each day,
And stop us fall prey to the easy way?
From early morning to late at night,
This cat makes our life fun and bright.
She waits for us to come home from shopping,
And sometimes she keeps us hopping.
As in and out she comes and goes,
Watch you don't step on her toes!

By closely watching our cat,
We are learning this and that.
It seems this cat has ESP,
How it works is a mystery!
She sensed when we had pain in heart,
brought us comfort, was real smart.
Peacefulness marks her whole life,
There is no unpleasant strife.
Another ability is her equanimity,
As well as the cat's calm serenity.

Yet she remains alert and aware,
Knows what goes on here and there.
The cat is funny just by being,
This we are both daily seeing!
She gives us reason for frequent laughter,
We always feel good thereafter.
She now has less spunk in the morning,
But without her, life would be boring!
This cat has a special presence.
A mysterious inner essence.

At four o'clock in the morning,
Well before each day's dawning,
The cat gently scratches at the door,
And a new cycle begins once more.
Sometimes it is well before four,
That the cat is scratching at the door.
Sleepily we ponder, 'Should we let her in?'
Showing some grace, we choose to let her win!
She's an extra special cat,
There is no doubt about that!

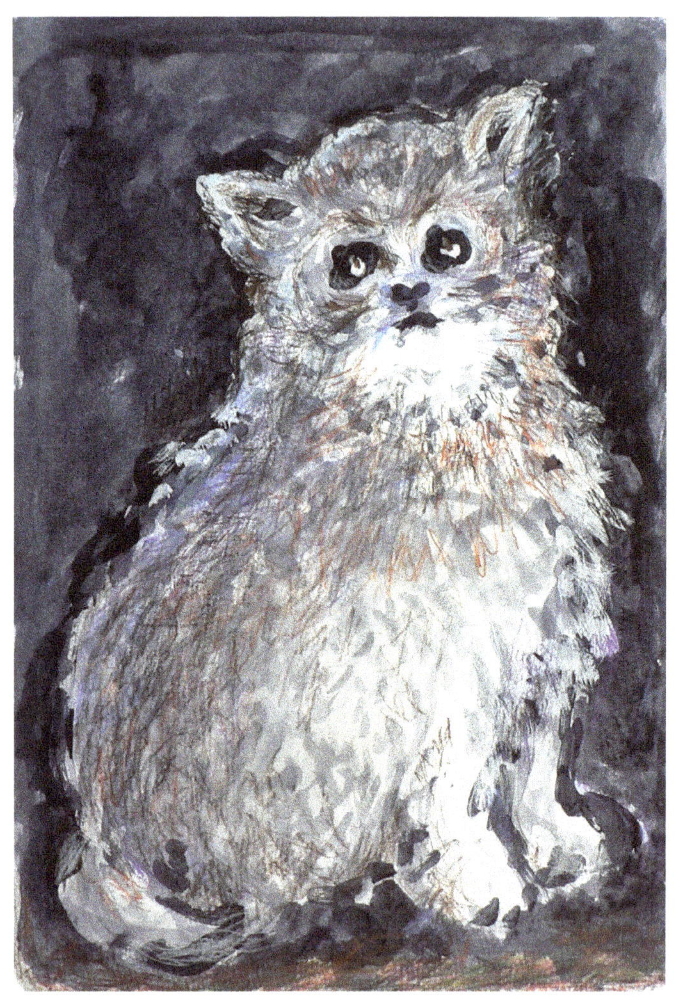

Mornings with Mikey

Very early in the morn,
Just after the crack of dawn,
Mikey sits at the balcony door,
Waiting for his snack on the floor.

Eva opens and hears his soft meowing;
This sweet visitor to pull on her heart strings allowing.
As over the horizon break the first rays of sunlight,
Time with Mikey on the balcony is a special delight.

Spending time with Mikey in quiet reflection,
Helps start off the day in the right direction!
Mikey is now the second early morning cat,
Who comes and waits on our front door mat!

Blackie's been coming and knocking on our screen door for years;
She brought us cheer at times when we were almost in tears.
That cat's spending more and more time here, and receives food;
Some cheese with a little meat and milk puts her in a good mood!

These two cats have been over time drawn to us,
Without, on our part, any intention or special fuss!
Mikey and Blackie are a study in contrast,
Their personality and taste differences are vast.

Mikey is always quiet, peaceful and calm,
His presence works on us like a healing balm.
Blackie is fretful and much more uptight,
Over little noises, she often gets a fright.

Mikey is the cutest, sweetest cat we have known;
Blackie is smart and has a mind of her own.
She is choosey and will not eat just anything;
Mikey cleans Blackie's leftovers and is grateful for everything.

Blackie gets jealous when we give Mikey affection,
She wants just for herself all the available attention.
Like a fierce dragon at Mikey she vents her displeasure.
But we love them both and think they're a treasure.

The daily presence of these two cats is a treat,
Two such faithful furry friends one doesn't often meet!
When the time comes for one or both of them to die,
It will bring us tears and a heavy, very sad sigh.

Yet, as Eva's father wisely tells us, 'Such is life'.
True, life does have ups and downs, and its strife.
"What happens to a pet after it dies?" people ask.
To answer such question is no quick and easy task!

It's hard to explain the nature of a cat or its essence,
But there's something special about these cats' presence!
We need to accept that some things are a mystery;
Over all knowledge, in this life, we do not have mastery.

We enjoy the friendship and faithfulness of these two cats,
Grateful for the experience, despite their occasional spats!
For the daily joy they bring us, to them we take off our hat,
Till such time that they no longer come to our front door mat.

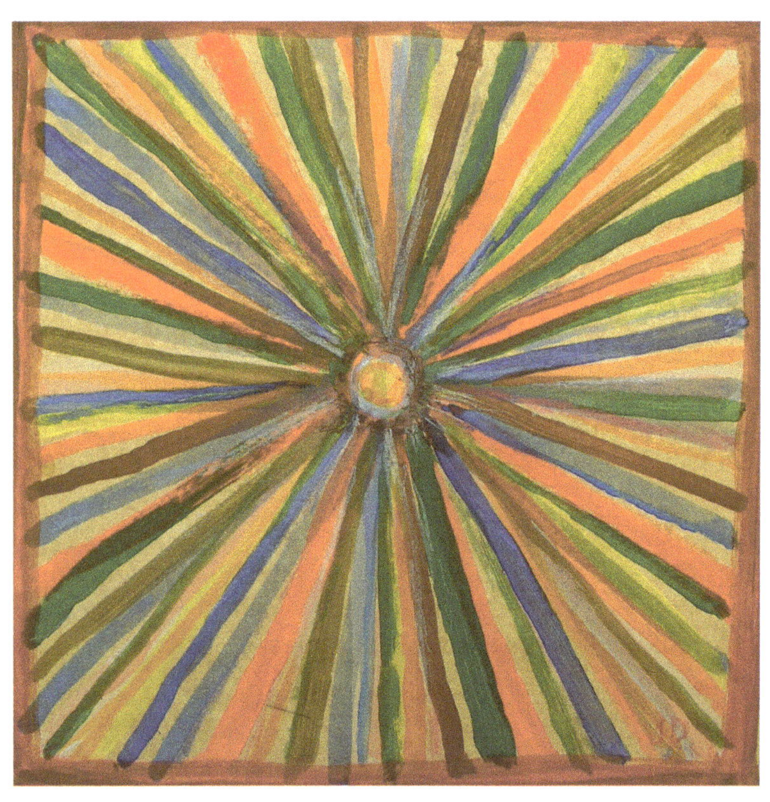

Hot Summer Days

The sky is blue and the sun is bright,
Makes all things a lovely sight.

The temperature is high,
Not a cloud in the sky.

For a walk it's far too hot,
We would come back totally shot.

We decide to go for a swim,
And it's not just on a whim.

So, we all dive into the pool,
And enjoy the water's pleasant cool.

Together we swim around and splash,
Enjoying the water with no clash.

After a while, we feel it's time out to go,
On the pool's edge, we exercise nice and slow.

Then, before too long, it's off to lunch,
To make us a contented bunch!

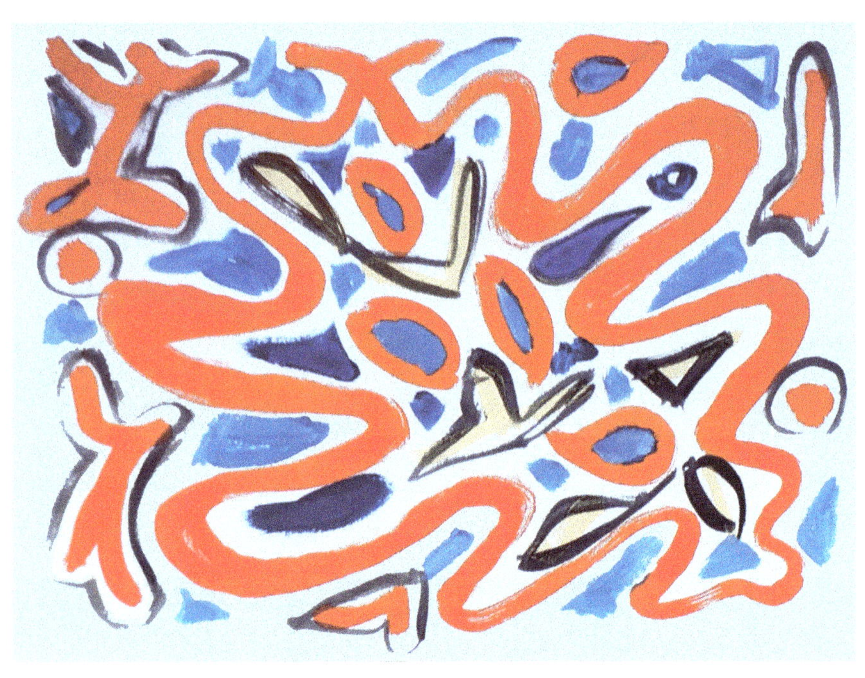

The Happy Children

With summertime, the grandkids are back,
Happily playing in the pool at the back.
Their joyful laughter's a delight to hear,
Great they have such fun, and not fear.

Soon it will be Christmas Day,
The children might be back to play,
Around their grandparents' pool,
Which on hot days keeps them cool.

Happy families are getting rare,
These kids are blessed to have such care.
May each child have a joyful life,
Live in a land without much strife.

It's good to hear the children play,
Adding delightful cheer today!

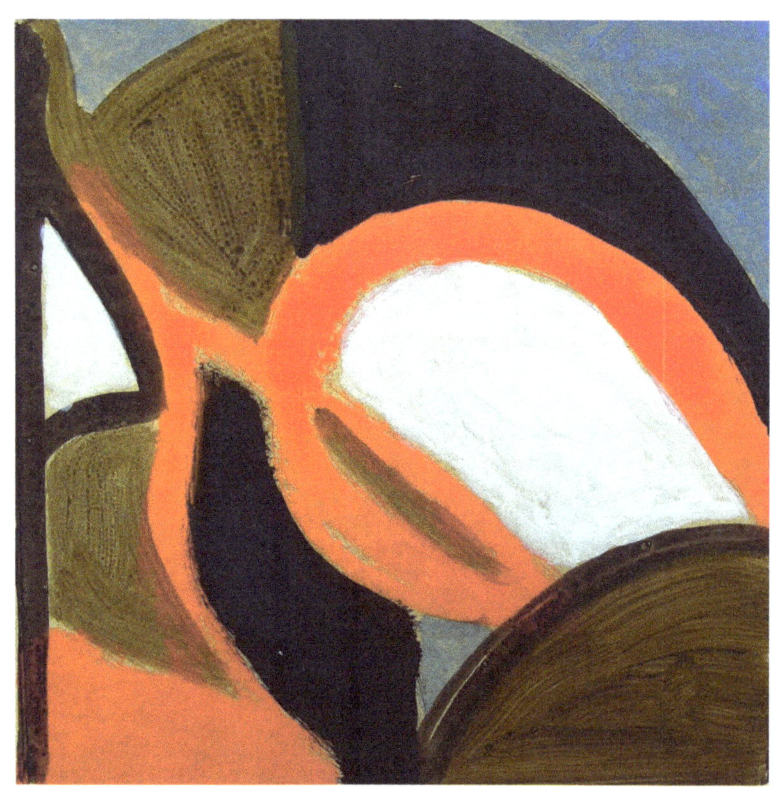

Almost-Burnt Toast

In looking for a tasty spread,
I forgot the toasting bread!
And then, to my shock and dread,
Smoke was rising from my bread!
If I keep losing my head,
Something worse could lie ahead!

So, make sure to keep your head,
Or, a disaster could lie ahead!
Multi-tasking tips you've been fed,
Which are leaving you misled!

By the wise, it has been said,
Do just one thing to get ahead.
Though you've been tempted and sped,
Such poor habits you need to shed!
So, at all times, keep your head,
To avoid the things you dread!

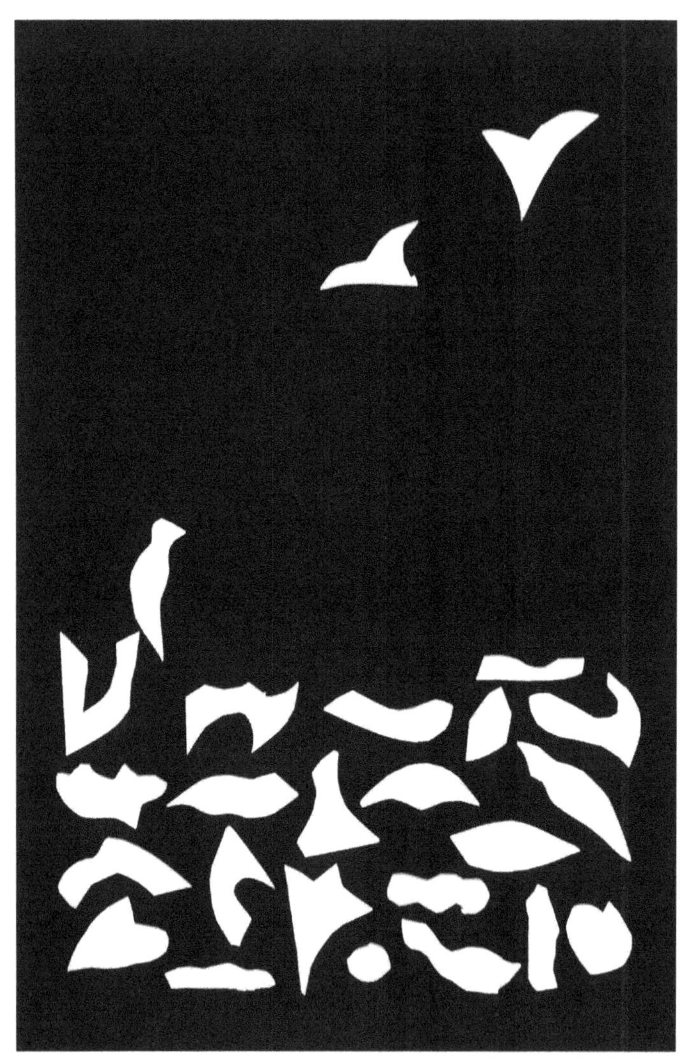

Balcony Bird Guests

From high up in their soaring flight,
Bird flocks on our balcony alight.
Early, at the break of light,
They bring a measure of delight.

One or two are now quite tame,
We throw to them crumbs as a game,
But also to their hunger assuage.
How long they stay, we cannot gauge.

Butcher birds wait on the window sill,
Patiently sit, sometimes quite still.
We enjoy every balcony guest,
And give each one of our best.

Year by year, the birds come and go,
Remind us of life's ebb and flow.
Days and nights . . . the time is fleeting,
Soon the end of life we'll be meeting.

"Carpe diem" says my father-in-law,
Wiser advice I rarely saw.
So, I'll let the birds continue to land,
While I get on with my tasks at hand!

Day by day, our life's ebbing away,
No-one's here to stay and just play.
We cannot know when our end will be,
So the future beyond we must clearly see.

Life can be like a wish-fulfilling jewel,
Not to make the most of it, you're a fool!
So let's not leave with nothing to show,
And in the next life down below!

To the birds I say "good-bye";
My, oh my, how the time does fly!

Epilogue

From Head to Heart

The nature of many of the poems may invite reflection and contemplation. In this context, these lines are offered:

You do not need to leave your room.
Remain sitting at your table and listen.
Do not even listen, simply wait;
Be quiet, still and solitary.
The world will freely offer itself to you to be unmasked;
It has no choice,
It will roll in ecstasy at your feet.

(Franz Kafka, 1883-1924)

In developing clarity and certainty at the heart level, the following three stages of understanding are also offered:

- Reading and studying; listening
- Reflecting or contemplating
- Meditating and integrating insights into one's being

Is Thinking about Death Morbid?

While working on the book, my father-in-law asked a question that we, too, had pondered earlier.

"Why are you focusing a lot on the end of life? You are still relatively young, active, and full of life – why do you have this sober focus in the book?" Here is an answer:

Several recent life experiences have drawn us to consider the end of life more earnestly.

After considering advice to arrange a pre-paid funeral plan, we were invited to visit a nearby crematorium and cemetery. The quiet peaceful bushland setting of the premises provides a poignant reminder of life and death. As we toured the manicured cemetery gardens, we were struck by the fact that there were tombstones for infants, children, youth, young adults, men and women in the prime of life, as well as older citizens. No one is exempt from the impermanence of life, and the age is not a determining factor!

For most of my life, I have intellectually accepted the fact that death is a certain reality for everyone. We may jokingly quip, "in life, only death and taxes are sure". However, this cemetery visit brought my understanding to the heart level – the realization that our duration of life is so uncertain. No one knows the exact time and circumstances of their death – life can unexpectedly end at any age.

Related questions began to emerge in my mind with more earnestness. What then is truly important in life? At the time of death, what is it that will help a person? It certainly will not be what they may have accumulated, struggled to acquire, and fought over. Even one's dearest family members, relatives, and friends will be unable to help prevent the final breath of life when the time comes.

In my Christian heritage and studies, end of life and death are distinct themes in the Scriptures. Equally, the afterlife is quite prominent. Later, in exploring Buddhism, I found that impermanence and death also feature noticeably.

There is evidence that there is a continuity of consciousness after we pass from this life. At death, the mind/spirit/soul separate from the body, which decomposes and returns to the earth, but a spirit component goes on. Consequently, the universal law of cause and effect continues to operate beyond our present lifespan!

All this has prompted a more serious view of life – especially being in my late sixties. Additionally, many other factors have merged.

An older family friend is presently struggling with advanced Parkinson's Disease. The end of life is unmistakably on his mind. Another family friend recently died from prostate cancer – we journeyed with him in his gallant struggle for the past three years.

Early in my life, I attended a small Christian college. Three fellow students have recently died – all roughly my age. Later in our career, my wife and I taught English as a foreign language overseas. Two of our colleagues have since died very unexpectedly – also roughly our age.

While death and dying are not subjects that everyone ponders (many may prefer not to talk about it, and just "live and let live"), nevertheless, death and the afterlife remain an important subject. People inevitably wonder, "What will happen to me one day?"

Further curiosity has arisen nowadays with near-death experiences, and research involving children looking at the possibility of past lives.

To me, the main issues involved are well expressed in words adapted from Peaceful Death, Joyful Rebirth, the introduction of which is entitled, "Death Is Not the End":

The day of death is the most crucial time for every person, universally. Whether you are from the East or the West, whatever your spiritual persuasion, or none – it makes no difference. The moment when consciousness departs from your body will be a momentous turning point of your life, for death will launch you on a journey into an unknown world. ...

Most people do not like to be reminded of their inevitable death, which may arrive at any moment. They are scared even to think about it, let alone discuss it. To some, the notion of contemplating death never even arises, absorbed as they are in the affairs of daily living. Although people of faith express confidence in an afterlife, many others insist that there is nothing at all after death. ...

The world's major religions agree that death is not the end, that "something" survives, although they differ in details and interpretation. Mind, consciousness, soul, spirit— whatever we call it— will continue to exist in one form or another. ... Though our bodies will dissolve back into the elements of which they are formed, we will continue as mind and consciousness, which will transmigrate into another existence." (From Tulku Thondup. *Peaceful Death, Joyful Rebirth*. Boston: Shambhala Publications, 2006.)

Far from being a morbid preoccupation, an awareness of impermanence, end of life, and death allows one to savour the precious opportunity of life to a far greater degree and meaningful extent. Every day, every hour, will then be cherished and used in the best way, rather than frivolously spent.

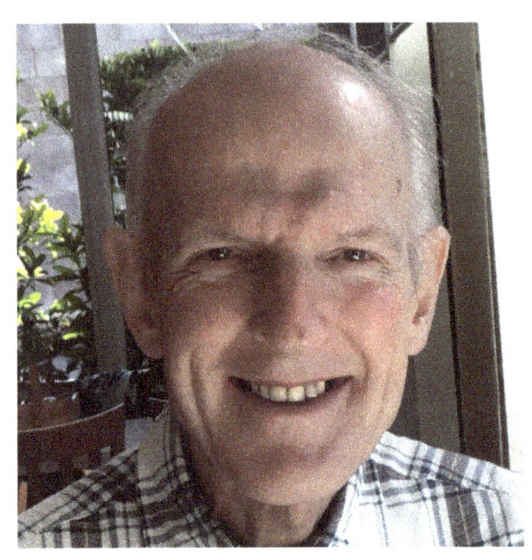

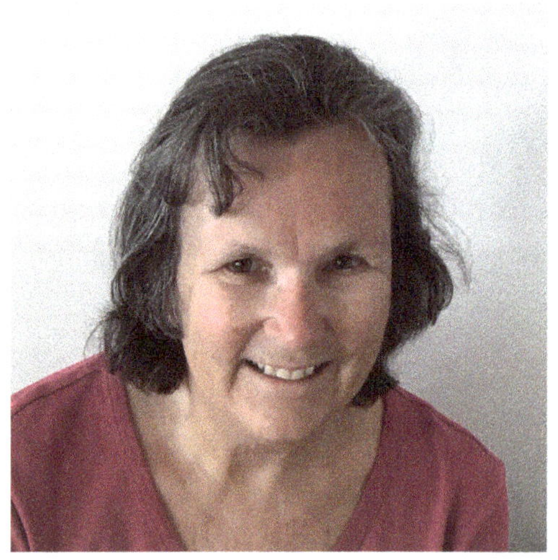

About the Authors

Alex and Eva Peck both come from families that had immigrated to Australia and settled in the state of Victoria. Alex arrived in Australia in 1950 with his parents (Swiss mother and Ukrainian father). Eva arrived in 1968 with her Czech parents, having lived in Sweden for two years, but grown up in the then Czechoslovakia.

After completing their tertiary studies in Australia, Alex and Eva had the opportunity to work together in the United States (1975-1993), Czech Republic (1993-2001), South Korea (2001-2005), and Saudi Arabia (2006). Their work included writing and editing, as well as teaching English as a foreign language. During this time, they also furthered their education in theology and education.

Their international experiences, including interaction with a variety of faith traditions and communities, have helped them to gain a broader and more inclusive perspective on spirituality.

In 2007, Alex and Eva returned to Australia and settled near Brisbane, in the state of Queensland. There they both gained Masters of Theology degrees.

They continue to explore and write in the area of spirituality, and have self-published several books and created a number of websites. Their other interests include reading, nature, walking, photography, and healthy living.

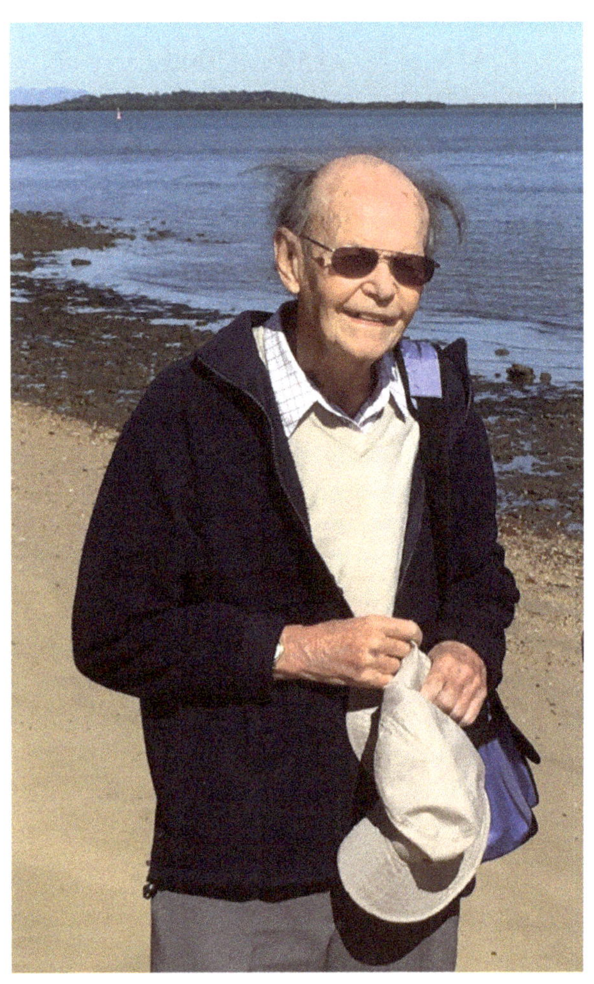

About the Artist

Jindrich (Henry) Degen was born in 1923 in Prague, Czechoslovakia, now the Czech Republic. Since his youth, he has been interested in both art and music. After his secondary education, he studied music and enrolled in the Prague Conservatorium Instrumental Section, specializing in the oboe. Following graduation, he worked for two decades in symphony and opera orchestras in Prague. When he and his family left Czechoslovakia, he performed for two years in the Great Theatre Orchestra, Gothenburg, Sweden. In 1968, Jindrich and his family immigrated to Australia, and for eleven years, he was the first oboe player in the Melbourne Symphony Orchestra in the state of Victoria.

After Jindrich's retirement in 1979, and move to the state of Queensland, he devoted himself to art. He has participated in different art groups, and is presently a member of Yurara Art Society in Redland City. He is very versatile, having done portraits, still lifes, nature, landscapes and a great variety of abstract and semi-abstract art, using different media. He has featured his works in several solo exhibitions at the Redland Art Galleries.

As an artist, Jindrich finds the Redland City environment conducive to expressing his feelings, responding to different light, colours and moods, and letting his imagination flow freely. Many of Jindrich's artworks can be seen on his website.

http://www.henrydegen.com